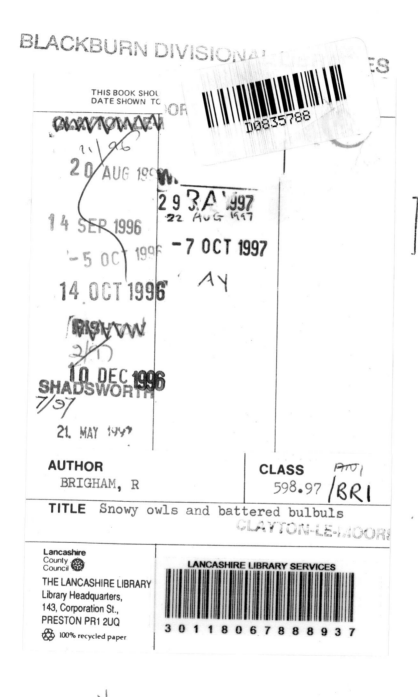

AUTHOR
BRIGHAM, R

CLASS
598.97 /BRI

TITLE Snowy owls and battered bulbuls

CLAYTON-LE-MOORS

SNOWY OWLS
AND
BATTERED BULBULS

Snowy Owls
and
Battered Bulbuls

Richard Brigham

ILLUSTRATED BY

John Paley

Whittet Books

First published 1996
Text © 1996 by Richard Brigham
Illustrations © 1996 by John Paley

Whittet Books Ltd, 18 Anley Road, London W14 OBY

British Library Cataloguing in Publication data.
A catalogue record for this book is available from the British Library.
ISBN 1 873580 27 4

Printed and bound by Bookcraft

CONTENTS

Dedication

To Trevor 'Munch' King, in appreciation of many soakings – both inside and out!

and

To Bob Holland, for pointing my bike in the right direction ...

1

OWLS IN THE OUTHOUSE

Skulking shapelessly in the far corner of the dimly illuminated rearing shed was a pair of grey, animated, pot-bellied powder puffs with glaring sulphur eyes; this gargoyle-like duo squeaked, hissed and booed in distinctly belligerent fashion.

Struggling through an accumulation of whirring incubators, glass-topped hatching units and abundantly populated rows of cages, we eventually got to the front wire of their temporary quarters. Energetically ducking and weaving their heads, the creatures reminded one of prize fighters dodging imaginary punches. We mutually inspected each other: what most impressed me was their size; I had expected something infinitely smaller.

When hatched they would have only been the size of diminutive day-old poultry chicks; now, five weeks later, the two young snowy owls had assumed the corpulent dimensions of half-grown cob chickens. In places the initial black-barred white feathers of juvenile plumage were already beginning to sprout through the thick layer of sooty-brown down previously enveloping their entire bodies.

One bird, slightly larger, darker, and of stalwart build, was evidently a female, for her first stubby feathers were more richly barred. By comparison, her brother was rather delicately composed, his body down much lighter and feathers slightly more advanced, particularly the flat facial disc of white feathers radiating from around the eyes, which gave him a gentle, deceptively benign appearance. In contrast, the female's hooded, heavily mascara-rimmed eyes and dark, scowling face made her look wickedly hostile. The look of unabashed defiance was exaggerated by the fact that she was panting in the afternoon heat, displaying to advantage the enormous gape of a viciously curved beak.

Regrettably, we had little time for more than a cursory inspection before resuming our journey. Without further ado the pair were manhandled into their travelling box, an operation that prompted much vigorous beak-clapping and a bout of the most pitiful squeaking. Negotiating once more the hazards of the rearing shed to an accompaniment of shrieking cockatiels, blaspheming parrots, and a miscellany of other feathered creatures that had by now taken up the cry, we emerged gratefully into the harsh glare of the

The snowy owl chicks were ducking and weaving their heads like a couple of prize fighters.

sun, and, with the box lid firmly closed, following an attempted break-out by the more athletic male, we took our leave for the journey home, our charges placed reverently between us on the front seat.

Earlier that day, Barbara, my long-suffering spouse, had agreed to accompany me on the expedition to Northamptonshire from our home in the heart of Norfolk. Having set out at noon on a blistering hot day, our travels took us across the wide open stretches of fenland to Lilford Park, a wildlife country park where the owlets had been hatched and hand-reared. It was a pleasant change to steal a few hours respite from the hectic, everyday life of a self-employed taxidermist. A taxidermist's life has many plus sides to it, not least of which are an unending source of interest, an exciting and satisfying way of scraping a living together, and also of fulfilling some artistic aspiration. Although it largely falls short in terms of cash incentive, we do manage to eat at reasonably regular intervals, and ample compensation comes from enjoying a life crammed absolutely full of interest and experience. Part of the enjoyment is unwittingly provided by a rich diversity of clients, for taxidermy is a profession that unfailingly attracts the more outrageous, unusual or eccentric characters. (None more so than one due to visit the following day, called Dimpton-Smythe.)

Dimpton-Smythe – Colonel, no less! – is regrettably one of the minuses. More specifically, his specimens are, for I have as yet to receive one for preservation in anything approaching reasonable condition. It is quite the norm for him to discover some mangled unfortunate creature on the road that has experienced a head-on collision with nothing short of an articulated lorry. Peeling it carefully from the tarmac, he stuffs it carelessly into a plastic bag for safe keeping. Instead of rushing the remains to me with all due haste, or at the very least consigning it to the deep freeze, he spends at least a week admiring the decomposing corpse until – even with his obvious absence of a sense of smell – the hapless beast ultimately contrives to make its presence felt and prompts him to deliver it.

The phone had rung just prior to our departure.

'Dimpton-Smythe here!' boomed the familiar voice. 'I've recently picked up a green woodpecker, and would like it preserved.'

'Recently picked up' in all probability meant sometime during the last fortnight or so. It was nothing short of a miracle that Barbara managed to forestall his visit until the next day.

Following a pleasant pub meal to break the journey, we had arrived at Lilford well before the appointed hour, spending an enjoyable interval inspecting the immaculate grounds and exhibits of the park that included over twenty species of owl, most impressive of which were a beautiful pair of great greys, of which there were only a limited number of pairs in the country; they are natives of the boreal coniferous zones of both Old and New Worlds. With massive facial discs and proportionately tiny yellow eyes, the pair stared back unblinking from the welcome shade of a gnarled log perch situated conveniently amongst a lush growth of trailing ivy, their buff-grey plumage subtly barred, flecked and striated with delicate grey-brown markings blending perfectly with the tree trunk on which they reposed.

A chorus of beak-snapping and and serpent-like hissing emanated from the box as the pick-up whirred into life, but by the time we had bumped our way along the pot-holed park drive to the open road, the birds had accustomed themselves to the noise and motion of the vehicle, at last settling down comfortably on an old pullover lining the base of the box, allowing the journey to be undertaken with only the occasional comment on my driving ability if I cornered too quickly, or was forced to apply the brakes. The return journey during the busiest part of the day seemed interminable, the heat turning the truck cab and travelling box into an oven. Every so often we carefully opened the lid to check our charges were not suffering unduly. Each inspection was greeted with hostile glances, the owlets apparently attempting to out-do each other in terms of disagreeable expression. More effective was the unholy stink they had joined forces to create in the airless confines of the vehicle.

Arriving safely home at last, the youngsters, by now panting wearily from the heat, were transferred from the box to the comparative coolness and fresh air of the large outhouse mews adjoining the house. Before allowing them to recover and familiarise themselves with their new surroundings, I hastily nailed a screen of weldmesh over a pane of glass shattered recently by son Michael in an apple-throwing dispute with his big sister, Jennifer.

I looked in on the owlets later before retiring to bed. Although I offered food, both birds were still in a minor state of disquiet and respectfully declined. I also suspected they were on the point of 'casting' – producing a pellet of waste feathers and bones. These are regurgitated regularly after the edible parts of an earlier meal have been fully digested.

Our latest acquisitions represented the culmination of four years of waiting: four patient years of hopes and fears, triumphs and disasters, since I had acquired a pair of snowy owls in the hope of fulfilling – or at least attempting to fulfil – a somewhat whimsical boyhood ambition: the training, flying and hunting of a snowy owl.

Living on a farm in a small Norfolk country village, from a tender age I had developed and nurtured a passionate interest in wildlife, especially bird-life and, in particular, birds of prey, who for me held an almost obsessional fascination. Partly it was due to their aloofness, pride and complete mastery of the air, the stealth and cunning of the hunter, and the fact that they held the power of life and death over lesser species with their capable hunting abilities. Not least it was due to the exciting fact that many species could be tamed, trained and ultimately used for hunting.

My adolescent spare time was spent working at a local wildlife park amongst a vast collection of birds and beasts; the park boasted the largest collection of European wildlife in the world and also the most comprehensive accumulation of exotic game birds in captivity. Of far more interest to me was the park's impressive collection of birds of prey.

Apart from a regal looking golden eagle that on special occasions I was entrusted to carry from the mews to his daily weathering block, my favourites were a magnificent pair of snowy owls, ensconced in a large, tastefully landscaped aviary. Like most owls, they appeared content to spend most of the daylight hours quietly on a bough in the corner of the enclosure, seldom induced to take wing except when fluttering laboriously to collect food from the aviary floor. Observing them regularly and intimately during my duties with many a covetous glance, I thought how wonderful it would be to see such a magnificent bird taking full advantage of its aerial powers, allowed to fly completely free as in the wild, and to be able to share with it the thrills of hunting. At the time, short of an inconceivable expedition to the far north, there was little I could do.

But now, by virtue of being self-employed, my extremely flexible working hours had allowed me time to gain a reasonable amount of first-hand experience in owl husbandry, the species concerned ranging widely from a diminutive little owl brought in, presumed dead, for preservation and mounting, to a huge female European eagle owl, weighing on the heavy side of 3.5 kilos (7.7lb).

The little owl was a road casualty suffering the effects of severe concussion and shock and was not expected to survive, but after two days of intensive care, during which it was painstakingly force-fed, our patience was rewarded when it recovered sufficiently to flit around our bedroom like an elusive will-o-the-wisp, disappearing frequently behind the curtains and peeping out periodically to fix us with a tiny pair of cross, piercing yellow eyes, waiting for a titbit to be produced.

A lady client had brought the bird into us; she had set her heart on having a stuffed owl for many years; when she duly turned up a few weeks later hoping to collect it, she was inconsolably put out by the news that the owl had made a complete recovery from its injuries. Having lost all fear of humans, the bird had been transported to the wildlife park to take part in a captive breeding project.

At the other end of the scale – quite literally – both in size and weight, was 'Gonk', the European eagle owl, so called for her juvenile resemblance to the quaint cuddly toys that became fashionable some years ago. She had been trained to fly free, and had gradually developed almost human traits to the extent that she liked nothing more than to accompany me virtually everywhere on the passenger seat of the truck as I went about my everyday business. Admittedly, most of our nocturnal excursions ended up at the local hotel, where close friend and fellow owl enthusiast, Munch, allegedly worked as head gardener. There, Gonk would regularly accompany me to the bar, perching her portly frame rather regally upon a plush bar stool and partaking of an occasional sip of best bitter, as if such mundane procedures were quite common practice amongst enlightened owl society.

Almost house-trained, only once did she demean herself, copiously blotting a previously untarnished copybook by lifting her tail and defecating deliberately and most profusely on the lounge carpet, an action that raised an eyebrow or two amongst the clientele, but left Gonk entirely unapologetic, peering below her innocently before staring accusingly along the bar as if in search of the culprit. A frantic search of my pockets revealed nothing more inspiring than half an ounce of tobacco, a virtually toothless hair comb and the remains of a dead rat, barely adequate instruments for such an emergency. Luckily, spending a fair proportion of his spare time propping up the bar, Munch disappeared smartly to the kitchen for a damp cloth with which to restore the carpet to its former well groomed condition.

The bar was packed solid when we arrived a few days later on a never to be forgotten evening. To avoid instigating a mass exodus of the hotel, I left Gonk to her own devices in the truck, but was finally persuaded to collect her, one particularly ardent owl enthusiast having come armed with her camera in anticipation of Gonk's appearance at some time during the evening. Having gained the bar through the centre of the crowd – a delightfully easy operation with an intimidating eagle owl on one's hand – we retired with a pint to the comfort of the settee in the far corner. Preening herself conceitedly as her admirer rushed off in a state of high excitement to collect her

Gonk would perch her portly frame regally on a bar stool.

camera, Gonk suddenly arched her wings and stretched her neck upwards. Leaning forward, her beak almost touching the glove, she shook her head, flamboyantly ejecting a gigantic casting; the ball of waste matter from her latest meal. The disgusting accumulation of chick fluff, rat fur and indigestible bones lay in a gently steaming and highly accusing mess at my feet. Mindful of attracting the attention of the resident diners tucking into sirloin and chips at the nearby table, I surreptitiously flicked the object from sight beneath the settee with my foot, intending to quietly pocket it later, as soon as the chance, and possibly a spare table napkin, arose.

The photographic session over, we settled for a quiet drink. By the end of the evening when the crowd had almost dispersed, the remaining clientele had developed what could be described as a moderately relaxed frame of mind.

One particularly eager beaver had in fact become so completely relaxed that he swayed almost on the point of semi-consciousness. As I went to refill my glass, he nearly slid off his corner seat as Gonk plonked herself importantly on the adjoining stool; she remained unruffled as the gentleman, who had at this late hour attained a semi-depressive state of mind, somewhat conspiratorially poured out his troubles to a philosophical, though apparently attentive ear.

Eventually, running out of what was an entirely one-sided conversation, her new-found friend suddenly came to his senses.

Following a disbelieving glance at his wristwatch, he drained his glass and rose hastily, if rather unsteadily, to his feet.

'What the hell am I going to tell my wife?' he slurred, making a somewhat futile attempt at standing. 'She'll never believe I've been sitting here all night, holding a conversation with a bloody great owl!'

Prudently allowing the gentleman a few minutes' grace, I also took my leave, forgetting completely about the casting flicked out of sight earlier, beneath the settee. By the time I remembered, it was far too late to return. I shuddered to think what the cleaner would make of it in the morning.

Soon after her arrival, Gonk ensured that the entire household rapidly learned a healthy respect towards owls. Jennifer and Michael were fully conversant with weird, if not always wonderful, creatures about the house, sensibly allocating any recent arrivals a comfortably wide berth. One half of the canine contingent, Whisper, the German short-haired pointer, was soon able to confirm that $3\frac{1}{2}$ kilos of irate eagle owl is an experience not to be taken lightly. The indignities of being pursued around the garden by such an adversary were certainly no laughing matter; Spider the cat also became swiftly and sufficiently adept at keeping at least the necessary one step ahead or Gonk would surely have eaten her.

And yet, Gonk could be so gentle. Her manner – towards me at least – at times bordered on affection as she gently nibbled my ear or teased absentmindedly at my beard while resting on the glove, the endearments administered with a beak that could sever an earlobe as easily as a virgin set of secateurs, tweeting and cooing so plaintively that one could be forgiven for regarding her as a great big, soft, cuddly toy, instead of an extremely powerful bird of prey capable of felling a moderately sized deer.

And thus, bearing past experience in mind, the unprecedented idea of attempting to train and hunt a snowy owl was perhaps not quite the eccentricity it seemed at first glance.

From a very tender age, falconry played a large part in my life; I got my very first kestrel, which was trained, largely by trial and error, to hunt crane flies and selected types of the larger winged beetles, at the age of seven.

Over the following years my hawking exploits progressed to the training, flying and hunting of buzzards and goshawks in pursuit of a wide range of quarry, the latter providing many a free meal in the shape of pheasants, rabbits, mallard, moorhen, geese and a host of rather less legitimate prey, taken around the farmland and marshes surrounding my home by this most elite of hunters. I shared many an adventure with a pair of goshawks, Venom and Rymattlya, flying each one daily to keep it fit and fast.

The goshawk, although somewhat cantankerous and moody, has been extensively used for falconry purposes for centuries; it roughly resembles the sparrowhawk in shape, colour and conformation, though it is many times larger. Swift, keen and a deadly hunter, the goshawk is a regular provider for the cooking pot, flown directly from the fist at quarry flushed before it, or, as I often preferred, cast off to a suitable vantage point well forward, to wait while quarry is disturbed from rough areas of ground hunted towards it. From its lofty position the bird is able to scan the ground minutely, often spotting the movements of prey well in advance of the falconer, and more than ready for the chase by the time the quarry is flushed.

From a standing start, the goshawk has a truly amazing take-off speed, easily capable of overhauling all but the swiftest of wing or the fleetest of foot. In complete contrast, the snowy owl is hardly an ideal candidate for falconry purposes, built neither for speed nor dexterity in the air, and positively cumbersome in build. As far as I could discover, there were no previous records of such a bird being successfully trained and flown for hunting, although I had heard of at least two attempts that failed miserably. Perhaps a trifle over-confident of my prowess and experience as a falconer, I therefore decided to be the first.

An eternal optimist, I could see no logical reason why the bird could not be trained and flown at quarry. The wild snowy obviously relies on its hunting skills for its very survival, proving itself a qualified predator of rabbits, rodents and the occasional bird, and capable of dealing with even the arctic hare, though its staple diet is the rather more humble and prolific lemming, the petite rodent that flourishes abundantly on its northern breeding grounds.

The snowy owl (*Nyctea scandiaca*) is undeniably one of the more spectacular species among the widely differing owl tribe. Comprising some 130-odd species worldwide, the family ranges from the diminutive elf owl of the southern United States and Mexico – barely more than sparrow size – to the aforementioned eagle owl, which can attain a weight of almost 4 kilos (9lb) and is capable of catching and dispatching small deer.

Although considerably lighter in weight, the female snowy appears only slightly smaller, measuring over half a metre (1.5 feet) from beak to tail and possessing an extended wingspan of around 140 centimetres (5 feet). In common with most owls, and indeed hawks and falcons, the female is by far the larger of the sexes. Darker in colour than the male, whose plumage is almost completely white apart from minimal amounts of black flecking, her plumage is heavily barred, flecked and spotted with dark brown, almost black markings. Largely diurnal, the snowy hunts by sight mainly during the daylight hours, when it captures prey in a pair of massive feet equipped with inch-long talons, its colossal strength sufficient to incapacitate anything up to and including an animal the size of an arctic hare. The feet and toes have evolved a dense covering of almost fur-like feathers, affording some measure of protection from the bitterly cold conditions in most of its territory.

The northernmost species of owl, the snowy occupies a vast circumpolar belt, north of the tree line, on the barren tundra regions, ranging from the snow and permafrost of the high arctic to its occasional southernmost boundaries of central Europe and the USA. Wandering over the vast, treeless northern expanses of tundra, it occupies a territory where prey is temporarily in abundance, nesting where an ample food supply can be exploited during the few brief weeks of comparative warmth of the arctic summer. The success or otherwise of breeding depends largely on the availability of lemmings – the small, hamster-like rodent, famed for its suicidal tendencies, which forms the staple diet of adults and nestlings alike. Lemming numbers vary dramatically from year to year, and, depending on the regular cyclic population explosions of the creature, the female snowy will accordingly produce a larger number of eggs, sometimes up to ten or more in a clutch. At such times the promiscuous male is said occasionally to indulge in polygamy, reputedly able to support two females and their young when food is in such abundance: a frequently observed habit amongst modern human society, it is possibly unique in the otherwise strictly monogamous world of owls.

2

CAREERING COLONELS

Next morning I awoke bright and early, with the strengthening sun streaming in through the bedroom window and bathing the country-side in its warming rays. The waters of West Lake twinkled brightly two hundred metres away, where a flotilla of greylag geese lay peacefully at anchor, and a snowstorm of black-headed gulls swirled lazily above the water. There was barely the faintest suggestion of a cloud in sight, the sky an unbroken thrush-egg blue, bringing the promise of yet another scorching day to add to the desiccating effects of a month-long drought.

Easing myself carefully out of bed to avoid disturbing Barbara's recumbent figure, I received a disapproving glance from Spider the cat, who yawned and stretched luxuriously before turning over and purring herself to sleep. Pausing only long enough to pull on my trousers, I left them to their dreams, tiptoeing downstairs and out of the back door to the mews, where the first dancing butterflies were already busy on the fragrant purple spikes of the buddleia bush, and a constant procession of house martins swooped back and forth to mud nests lodged beneath the eaves. Creeping quietly to the mews window – courtesy of Michael's recent inaccuracy – I was afforded a clear view through the broken window pane.

Both owlets were snuggled cosily together like a huge ball of fluff in the far corner, lying flat out on their tummies, eyes tightly closed, completely relaxed and apparently dead to the world apart from tiny regular nodding movements of their heads.

They heard the footsteps on the gravel path as I retraced my steps, and on opening the door, I was greeted by insistent begging cries for food as the pair advanced in a nimble, high-stepping, penguin-like gait, displaying no lack of self-confidence, beaks pulling and nibbling at my trousers while insisting to be fed. A systematic search of the floor revealed two fresh castings amongst the wood shavings: large, neat and compact bundles of waste feathers and indigestible material from their last meal. Both were firm but moist with no unpleasant odours, a good indication that all was well internally.

Fulfilling my new role of foster-mother, I offered the female a chick. It was snatched greedily, and forcefully crammed down whole amid much neck-

16

stretching and gulping, her eyes closing momentarily as the chick's rear extremities finally disappeared. So much for etiquette or table manners. The male followed suit, both birds accepting two whole chicks before their solicitings weakened. The offer of a third was somewhat condescendingly accepted, prior to each bird retreating to a separate corner of the mews, where each placed its prize with much reverence and minor adjustment, presumably to be consumed later in a more leisurely fashion and with rather more decorum. Further offers of food were totally ignored, the owlets settling down comfortably amongst the deep wood shavings, eyes half closed and clicking their beaks in polite refusal.

It was my first real opportunity to inspect my charges in more detail. Their feathering was developing rapidly: copious amounts of grey body down were gradually being shed, to be replaced by the black-barred, white attire of their first juvenile plumage. When first hatched, the snowy owl chick is covered rather sparsely in pure white down, as soft and velvety as a mole. This is gradually replaced by a much thicker layer of dark grey, presumably to allow absorption of as much as possible of the sun's warmth in its normal arctic nursery, retaining body heat during the later stages of the chick's development, when the female is unable to cover her rapidly growing brood adequately, and spends more time away from the nest performing her share of the hunting duties, instead of brooding constantly as in the early days of the owlet's life.

The growing feathers were far more noticeable on their backs and wings, the remainder of the body cloaked in the thick layer of down, more copious at the top of the legs, which gave each one the impression of a pair of rather ill-fitting plus fours. A stubby little apology of a tail protruded stiffly backwards, barely 7 centimetres (3 in.) long and heavily barred with black. The layer of wispy white face feathers contrasted with a black moustache of hairlike tufts, protruding each side of the strong, viciously curved beak. The female, lacking the light grey face of her brother, appeared to be wearing black-rimmed spectacles, which did nothing to soften her severe, scholastic, almost menacing appearance. Whatever her mood, I suspected she could do little towards transforming her facial expression to look anything other than positively murderous.

Feeding time over, I set out to check a line of snares set recently along the edge of a nearby cornfield, hoping I could vary the owlets' diet with a taste of fresh rabbit. Rabbits being rabbits, there had been something of a local population explosion earlier in the summer, and a field of barley bordering a rough copse a field away from the house had suffered severe damage, the stalks nibbled and trodden to ground level over almost an acre of ground. During the previous week, I had taken well over forty rabbits from two dozen snares. Sure enough, as I did my rounds with the skylarks trilling in the heavens, and the sun warm on my bare back beginning to burn off the early morning dew, I collected three more taken during the short hours of darkness: clean, healthy and luckily spared the agony of myxomatosis, the man-made plague that takes a cruel toll with monotonous regularity when their numbers are high, wasting good meat and inflicting a long, painful and lingering death to those afflicted.

Having returned home and prepared the rabbits – one for the owlets and a brace for the kitchen – I attended to the needs of the diverse collection of livestock that shares our home, feeding and watering the many mouths before attending to my breakfast. The early morning feed round is no mean task, the confines of the house and garden host to all manner of creatures from gerbils to German pointers, carp to cockatiels, though for the most part composed of web-footed fowl, my most time-consuming hobby being the keeping and breeding of wild ornamental waterfowl from around the world. The truly cosmopolitan collection includes gorgeous mandarin ducks from China, dainty red-breasted geese from Siberia and smew from the far, cold north, hooded mergansers from North America, Argentine ruddy ducks, Bahama pintail, Pacific brent and Hawaiian geese, the latter duo penned discreetly alone and headed by a sadistic old gander who metes out punishment in the form of a severe trouncing, inflicted indiscriminately upon anyone or anything foolish enough to trespass within his pen in the springtime, when the task of guarding his breeding territory weighs heavily on his mind. At such times his attentions extend not least of all to his timid spouse, who, stepping out of line, is liable to be abused in the same undiscerning manner. Being something of a masochist, she remains utterly and unshakeably faithful, each year producing an endearing clutch of his fluffy grey goslings.

Two dogs, a cat, a gerbil, aviaries of cockatiels, parrots, parakeets, owls and canaries, a flock of geese, a collection of ducks and a pondful of fish form the resident nucleus of the collection, their numbers supplemented each summer by youngsters which can total anything up to two hundred, all having to be fed, watered, let in, let out, caught up, let go and maintained in a reasonable state of health and hygiene. The various morning tasks of tending such a flock are accompanied by a veritable orchestra of shrieks, whistles, cackles, quacks, hoots, chirps and trillings, swearing and intermittent barking, as the dogs give an impatient reminder that it is time for an early morning romp across the fields. The pen of rapidly growing red-breasted goslings requires moving daily to pastures new, the birds consuming vast areas of grass like an octet of animated lawn mowers. Last, but by no means least, the inmates of the various owl aviaries at the top of the garden are patiently waiting to be fed. It comes as something of a relief when all is done, and I can at last attend to my own breakfast. At least the spell of early morning activity promotes a good appetite. As my old waterfowl breeder friend, Trevor, quite succinctly put it, during one of his frequently recurring attacks of acute depression:

'If you didn't have to feed one end, and clear up behind the other, this job would be bloody easy!' Never a truer word has been spoken.

The early morning ritual over, I met Barbara at the back door. She had just returned from an energetic spell of dog walking and, milk jug and udder cloth in hand, was about to dispute ownership with Tina the goat regarding the daily supply of milk.

'Oh, what a pity,' she quipped in mock sympathy, 'You've just missed your dear friend, Colonel Dimpton-Smythe, on the phone. He just rang to inform you to expect him around lunchtime.'

Groaning inwardly, I reflected that there just had to be something to spoil such a beautiful morning.

Breakfast quickly dispensed with, I placed the owlets in their travelling box, and, with Barbara safely out of the way ferrying the children to school, sneaked them upstairs to my study, where I was to spend the morning editing material for a forthcoming waterfowl book, now – mercifully – almost complete. That way I could keep an eye on them, enabling the three of us to get to know one another rather more intimately, besides providing a little light relief while contemplating the dubious pleasure of Dimpton-Smythe's arrival. At least it seemed a good idea at the time.

Placing the box on the desk beside the window, I settled myself and attempted to compose a readable sentence or two. It was far from easy with the continual distraction of a pair of inquisitive woolly heads bobbing up and down like a double-barrelled jack-in-the-box, as the double act studiously examined the house martins, whizzing to and from their nests above the study window with cargoes of insects, or turned to stare at me with scornful, penetrating eyes. Each time I glanced up from my work, one or other of the birds met my eye, staring rather rudely and unapologetically until I returned the gaze, when it would disappear rapidly below the rim of the box as if in mock embarrassment..

Worse was to follow. Having eventually decided that writing was vastly over-rated as a spectator sport, the owlets finally settled down for a mid-morning nap, allowing me at last to make some progress. With the rough draft completed, I switched the pen for the typewriter, the action prompting an immediate reaction from the depths of the box, whose inmates now really went to town, my initial tappings on the keyboard accompanied by frenzied and quite sustained bouts of beak-clapping from within the box, the two heads reappearing instantly I applied myself to the task. My normal typing speed is certainly nothing to write home about, but with the three of us tapping away with machine-gun rapidity, the bedlam emanating from the study doubtless gave the impression that my word per minute output had increased dramatically, our combined efforts sounding most impressive, though total output suffered greatly. It was comical at first, though utterly impossible to concentrate under such pressures, and by the third page the accompaniment had become a trifle monotonous, each pause and new paragraph greeted with a renewed volley of energetic clattering.

Above the racket my ears were constantly attuned for the deafening roar

Our combined efforts sounded most impressive.

of a vehicle that would announce the imminent arrival of Dimpton-Smythe. 'Around lunchtime', judging by previous experience, could quite easily mean any time between eleven thirty and half-past three, the colonel obviously flexible regarding mealtimes. Sure enough, just prior to mid-day, the unmistakeable scream of an engine and the spatter of flying gravel signalled his touchdown on the front drive, the vehicle careering past the front porch and grinding to a dusty halt only millimetres short of the wall. With his boot remaining stubbornly flat on the floorboards, the engine continued to revolve at full tilt for several seconds until he most thoughtfully switched it off, and the hallowed silence of the surrounding countryside returned.

Allowing sufficient time for the dust to settle, the colonel decanted himself and purposefully ascended the front steps, a suspicious looking package, apparently concealing the expired woodpecker, bundled irreverently under his arm.

The formalities over, I ushered my guest into the workshop to examine his latest specimen, slapped carelessly on the table with about as much care and respect one would show towards half a kilo of pork sausages. A paper bag and eight sheets of newspaper did little to conceal the smell, the last sheet of which had firmly adhered to an open wound.

'It's rather a pity I couldn't have brought it yesterday,' he announced, in mildly accusing fashion. 'It was in really good condition. With the temperatures we had last night, it seems to have deteriorated somewhat ...' Tailing off the statement with an icy glare ensured that there would be no doubt where the blame would lie, if, when he eventually turned up to collect it, the specimen was anything less than pristine and feather-perfect. It seemed of little use to remind him, yet again, to pop everything he found into the deep freeze immediately.

I could only agree, however, with his assessment, as I sorrowfully examined the mummified remains of what had once been a gorgeous male specimen of *Picus viridis*, reflecting sadly that the latest in a long line of the colonel's casualties was roughly par for the course. Doubtless in 'really good condition' approximately ten days ago, constant handling, continuous hot weather and a swarm of pregnant bluebottles had done their worst. The woodpecker was an object of beauty no more, in need of urgent attention if anything of its former glory was to be restored.

I also discovered an unsightly patch of feathers missing from its rump, probably removed upon impact by the vehicle with which it had originally collided. When I rather tentatively pointed this out, the colonel glared long and accusingly, as if I had removed the offending feathers and surreptitiously secreted them about my person. Allowing me sufficient time to own up, his subsequent exhaustive search of the mountains of newspaper failed to bring the misplaced feathers to light. I somehow managed to keep my tongue under control, and promised faithfully to do my best, at the same time steering him back to his waiting vehicle.

I spent the next three quarters of an hour picking fly eggs from the woodpecker corpse with a pair of eyebrow tweezers; there were plenty of them, grouped together in neat white rows, inside the beak, under the eyelids, and lodged stubbornly in the more intimate clefts of its anatomy. Finally, almost overcome with boredom, I consigned the bird to the deep freeze to put paid to any overlooked eggs.

Barbara, diplomatically out of the way for the duration of the colonel's visit, was no better pleased by it. The keen gardener of the family, she duly returned from a leisurely walk with Whisper, gaping disbelievingly at where my efforts to conceal the fresh, five metre scar along the edge of the carefully-tended lawn had been largely unsuccessful.

'I wish that old devil would either learn to drive, or get a smaller car,' she cursed vindictively. 'That's the third time he's run over my bloody grass!'

Thanking our lucky stars that at least the colonel hadn't turned up in a tank, we retired for a late lunch.

By mid-afternoon, my study had become stuffy and claustrophobic.

I returned the owlets to the mews, where it was far cooler out of the sun, and tried to work outside. Even so any progress was repeatedly distracted by a continuous stream of butterflies visiting the garden buddleia, and an intermittent procession of visitors to see the owls, whose dozing in the cool mews were interrupted spasmodically by a succession of pokings, proddings, strokings, fondlings and exclamations of delight.

The air was blissfully cool by the time my work was complete. Allowing the owlets the freedom of the back garden, I took the opportunity to get a few photographs as the inquisitive pair inspected the lawns and shrubberies in some detail, trundling comically around the garden in exaggerated goose-steps as if negotiating an icy surface, tripping over their own oversized feet or any minor obstacle in their path, and collapsing periodically in undignified heaps. It was here they were formally introduced to Whisper, the German pointer, a superb pedigree specimen of a bitch who is trained to work with gun and hawk, but who, besides possessing a comprehensive list of other, equally doubtful attributes, is an ardent purloiner of toilet rolls and bars of soap, which she pinches from the bathroom with increasing regularity and consumes with obvious relish. Many an urgent plea has emanated from the smallest room in the house, an unlucky occupant caught – quite literally – with their trousers down following a timely Whisper raid. It's not just toilet rolls: clothes pegs, empty crisp packets, the morning mail, plastic biros, the children's school homework and once, incredibly, one of Barbara's washing up gloves – all have a fascination for Whisper.

The latter reappeared a full day later, still intact, causing no little concern as a single pink finger appeared from Whisper's rear orifice to point somewhat accusingly at the ground. A pointer is normally renowned for pointing with its front end, specifically its nose, but, as Barbara was quick to mention, we had, quite uniquely, one that could point at both ends in two different directions simultaneously. From that moment on, 'pointer' took on a new meaning. To our extreme relief, and obviously Whisper's, the remainder of the glove followed in due course, but I must emphasise that it was never again used for washing up.

Whisper's faithful sidekick, Muttley, a mongrel of doubtful lineage, was also hovering quietly in the background. A dog of the sweetest nature who would refuse to harm a fly, the poor little fellow had come about as the somewhat bizarre result of an inadvertent and quite unimaginable rendezvous between a Labrador cross Alsatian, and a whippet cross dachshund, though he has far fewer vices than Whisper. With hardly an untoward thought in his head, Muttley's main downfalls are a severe affliction of halitosis, and an unwitting ability to look extremely sheepish when voices are raised, thereby arousing and inviting suspicion of misdeed. On such occasions he customarily deposits a little puddle on the kitchen floor and sneaks away to hide, head lowered submissively, tail at half mast and feet dragging heavily on the ground, assuming all the cares of the world at once on his rather less than broad shoulders.

The canine companions were unanimous in their disapproval of the owlets, both respectfully declining an intimate introduction with a distinct 'you must be joking' look, although by now quite used to passing acquaintanceship with all manner of weird and wonderful creatures that seem to turn up with monotonous frequency to share our home. True to form, the introductions over, Muttley slunk away unobtrusively with his tail between his legs, though Whisper paused to taste the air and point the new arrivals.

Whisper paused to point the new arrivals.

Minus the rubber glove on this occasion, she held point from a discreet distance, fully aware of the disadvantages of getting on too intimate a footing with any bird of prey. Having sniffed and scented to her satisfaction, she sneaked quietly away to see what she could steal indoors, lurking with probable intent at her vantage spot suspiciously near the bathroom.

Before returning them to the mews, with Barbara's help I carefully weighed and measured each owlet in turn. The female weighed just short of 1100 grammes (2lb.6oz.), slightly heavier than her brother, who tipped the scale at one kilo (2lb.2oz.) precisely. Both measured 37.5 centimetres (15in.) from beak to tail, although the female's wing was slightly longer, extending a full 45 centimetres (17.5in.) from body to tip and giving a total wingspan of over a metre (3 feet) in all. For fledglings a mere five weeks of age, the statistics seemed quite amazing, though rapid growth is a necessity of being reared naturally during the brief arctic summer, when time is of the essence and it is imperative for the bird to become fully mobile in the shortest possible time.

In the evening, each took two chicks followed by a few appetising chunks of fresh rabbit, which we shared as an evening meal. Fully replete, they settled down comfortably with eyes half closed to doze. When I looked in later to check them before retiring to bed, the light bulb had blown. Returning with the flashlight, I discovered both owlets once more wide awake and energetic, scrutinising their moving shadows cast on the wall from the beam of the torch, the appearance of which prompted closer inspection with bobbing heads until, apparently satisfied that the ghostly black monsters of the mews meant them no harm, they nestled cosily together in the soft bed of deep wood shavings covering the floor, and quietly went to sleep.

3

MATRIMONIAL MANOEUVRES

We had acquired the parent birds four years previously. Being an ardent keeper and breeder of ornamental waterfowl, I hatch and rear each season a surplus number of youngsters for sale, the majority of which are disposed of in the autumn to a professional breeder friend. Almost by accident, he had found himself with a surplus pair of snowy owls on his hands.

Totally unrelated, the birds were obviously ideal for a breeding project; one had been imported from Stockholm zoo in Sweden, the other originated in Canada. Realising they were consuming expensive food at an alarming rate, Trevor, quite capable of selling a secondhand fridge/freezer to an Eskimo, began to work on me immediately. I needed very little persuasion to relieve him of his worries – such an opportunity seemed far too good to dismiss.

Agreeing to accept the pair in part exchange for a consignment of waterfowl I had recently delivered, work began immediately on the drawing up of plans for a large aviary in the centre of the back garden. Assisted by a builder friend, the task was no sooner said than done, an aviary of sizeable dimensions appearing almost overnight, complete with a palatial roosting shed, a selection of nesting sites and shelters and various boughs, tree trunks and branches erected tastefully about the enclosure which, for aesthetic and concealment purposes, was duly planted up with a choice selection of miniature conifers. The added luxury of a sunken bath was also installed, enabling the owls to carry out the necessary ablutions for maintaining their plumage in pristine condition.

Barbara was absolutely dumbstruck, for, as she rather succinctly put it, the pine shelf in the kitchen still awaited erection after at least three years of asking, the loo seat remained in imminent danger of collapse, and even a menial five-minute shelving job in the airing cupboard had been quite blatantly overlooked. Aviaries, apparently, were a different story, even those of approximately one hundred and twenty cubic metres, fully landscaped and containing every modern convenience but the proverbial kitchen sink. Such things, it seemed, were inclined to spring up miraculously in the manner of a dawn mushroom on a dewy September morning.

Father-in-law, Alan, was inclined to agree. Something of a do-it-yourself fanatic, he regularly comments in passing upon the little jobs about the house that have been 'temporarily shelved', while other less conventional ideas are pursued with much vigour for little or no apparent purpose. My time could clearly be more gainfully employed.

Each time he plucks up sufficient courage to pay a visit, Alan unfailingly gets allotted the broken dining room chair I have been threatening to mend for some months, and during lunch is inclined to collapse in a heap of splintered wood halfway through his bakewell tart or prunes and custard, all for lack of the 'spot of glue' such a minor repair would warrant.

Father-in-law's last visit was a real nightmare, though he luckily manages to retain a sense of humour. Having routinely demolished his favourite chair during lunch, he was standing safely clear of the remaining furniture, when Barbara presented him with his birthday present, a brand new pipe bowl; almost salivating at the very thought of burning it in that very evening, he placed it reverently on the table as Barbara halved a freshly baked chocolate cake – his favourite – for him to take home, leaving it on the kitchen work top before escorting him on a light constitutional around the garden.

Returning a few minutes later, I met Alan in the kitchen, when he popped back into the house to collect his gifts before setting off for home.

'Have you seen my new pipe bowl?' he inquired, patting his jacket pockets absentmindedly, though displaying signs of agitation. 'I left it safely on the dining table with the wrapping paper. It can't be far away ... though ... funnily enough ... there's no sign of the paper ...'

A full ten minutes of combined searching discovered just about everywhere that the missing pipe bowl definitely wasn't. With nowhere left to look, by some elementary deduction, I began to suspect that yet another minor disaster had befallen poor old Alan, my worst fears realised when Barbara reappeared to confirm that she had cleared up the wrapping paper and thrown it on the kitchen stove, together, apparently with Alan's prize pipe.

'I DON'T believe it!' he bellowed, as Barbara began poking meditatively, but somewhat abortively, amongst the embers of the stove, clearly rather less than keen to unearth anything of an incriminating nature. 'On the other hand – YES! – I DO believe it!' he continued. 'That's bloody typical of this place. Give you something with one hand, and take it away with the other. Ye Gods, what a bloody madhouse!'

Itching to leave before something equally drastic should befall him, he went to collect his chocolate cake. Unfortunately, during his short absence, Whisper had beaten him to it. Apart from a few widespread crumbs and a smug expression on Whisper's face, very little evidence remained of Barbara's sumptuous creation.

'NOW ME BLOODY CAKE'S DISAPPEARED!' he stammered disbelievingly in his rich northern accent. 'I'll give you ten to one that ruddy mongrel's eaten it. That'll teach you to look after it' he added resignedly to himself.

By the way of consolation, Barbara managed to produce a further, significantly reduced, portion of chocolate cake. Without daring to take his hands off it this time, he prepared once more to leave, remaining in the doorway just long enough to sum up the situation. At least he saw the funny side.

'This place – at best – is a nightmare.' he confirmed. 'It's like an accident waiting to happen. Even the furniture jumps out to grab you. Put anything down in here, and either the parrot chews it to shreds, the flaming dog eats it, a bird craps all over it, or, failing that, Barbara throws it on the bloody fire.'

Retaining an adequate stranglehold on his small wedge of chocolate cake, he departed in haste while the going was moderately good.

However, to return to snowy owl matters. Despite a burning ambition to train such a bird, I harboured no intention of attempting one of the adults. The ultimate objective was to induce the pair to breed and produce a youngster for training, which would become 'imprinted' during the process of hand-rearing; this would aid the ultimate training programme. Imprinting is the normal outcome of a hand-reared bird; when it is fed exclusively by the human hand, it eventually regards its keeper as combined parent, provider and panderer to its every whim. With careful treatment, the creature's instinctive fear of humans is quickly dispelled.

Reared naturally by its parents, a wild youngster has first to be tamed – in falconry parlance, 'manned', before the actual training process can begin. An imprinted bird, however, is not without its drawbacks. I once, literally, shared the thrills and spills of hunting with a completely fearless buzzard, who, although parent-reared in an aviary and extremely wild and unmanageable when I first took her up for training, for some strange reason still became hopelessly imprinted on me.

After three weeks of concerted training, 'Spectre' quickly lost all inhibitions regarding the entire human race, which she regarded with so relaxed an attitude that it bordered almost upon contempt. As I normally work my hawks alone – unless Barbara accompanies me as unpaid beater and general dogsbody – at first, this appeared something of an advantage. Gradually, Spectre began to take liberties while being flown. Her set party piece, when my mind was occupied elsewhere, was to swoop from an unexpected quarter to snatch my hat before I saw her coming, a skilful feat requiring the deftest of footwork and flying expertise, but one accomplished with consummate ease. Clenched firmly in her talons, the hat was then conveyed triumphantly to the nearest vantage point, well out of reach. Alighting on the house roof, a handy telegraph pole, or the nearest tall tree, she took

She took great delight in ripping my hat to shreds.

great delight in methodically ripping my hat to shreds until, in desperation, I was forced to offer food in the hope of enticing her down. Often, much to the amusement of family and visitors alike, she tired of the 'game', abandoning my hat on the ridge tiles; it was then either a matter of taking potshots with the air rifle, in the hope of dislodging it, or, rather less simply, risking life and limb by scaling the slippery, moss-covered roof slates leading to the ridge. Either way, spectators were assured of an exciting performance.

Over the course of a few weeks, her antics almost completely destroyed my favourite hat, though on the whole it was quite an amusing trick, until one day she completely misjudged a particularly ambitious manoeuvre. Oblivious of her approach, I turned round at the culmination of a cunning rearward stoop and was struck squarely in the face. The resulting collision knocked me to the ground and sent Spectre erratically off course, her interrupted dive ending somewhat ingloriously in the nearest bramble bush. With ears singing and small rivulets of blood streaming down my face, the experience was on a par with being smacked in the face with a medium sized baseball bat.

Luckily, after cleaning up, I counted myself fortunate to escape with no injury more permanent than a profusely bleeding nose, a ripped earlobe, a cut lip, and a deep and disturbing gash just below my right eye. Spectre experienced the loss of a few feathers. From that moment on, I monitored her movements rather more carefully whenever she was in one of her 'playful' moods, and took swift evasive action whenever appropriate.

However, all in all the delights of flying and hunting with such an amenable bird far outweighed the occasional contretemps. Spectre would follow me virtually anywhere on our regular evening walks to the neighbouring village, trailing along the road from tree to tree, or to the top of telegraph poles and other suitable vantage points. Alternatively, she would take advantage of a warm thermal to soar effortlessly hundreds of feet above, playing on the wind, needing only a call for her to return in a breathtaking stoop to the glove. Reaching the outskirts of the village, her progress was from rooftop to rooftop, though I would disown her occasionally after glancing up to see a portly frame swaying rather ridiculously on a television aerial, to the equal consternation of the local house sparrows, and those viewing the 'box' inside.

Although the prospect of a full-grown snowy owl hitting one full in the face would, admittedly, be more than a trifle daunting, imprinting would at least overcome many of the bird's initial inbuilt fears. It would then require gradual introduction to other potentially alarming objects: dogs, cattle, motor vehicles and farm machinery, in fact virtually anything liable to be encountered when the bird was flown free, when sudden confrontation with any alarming object could, at worst, mean a terrified bird disappearing over the far horizon, possibly never to be seen again.

With the aviary construction work completed, I arranged to collect its new tenants. They were temporarily housed in a comparatively small aviary, with barely room to swing the proverbial cat, let alone wield a catching net. Trevor, their keeper, most thoughtfully allowed me the somewhat dubious pleasure of catching them up, foregoing the experience by ushering me all too unselfishly through the aviary gate armed with nothing more enterprising than a large plastic bucket, stationing himself strategically to keep careful watch from outside. The plan of action, I was instructed, was to entice each bird down to the aviary floor, creep to within suitable bucket-wielding range and surreptitiously slip the receptacle over the bird's head, disabling it sufficiently to steer it into the travelling box. According to Trevor, there was really nothing to it, simply a more stimulating version of 'pick your own', only rather more precarious.

The little male was reasonably co-operative. Despite a moderate amount of hissing and swearing, he allowed the bucket to be slipped over his head with relative ease. Thus encapsulated, with only a pair of feathery feet visible below the rim of the upturned bucket, he was unable to retaliate, and was marched into the box like a souped-up version of a giant Galapagos tortoise.

The female proved rather less amenable, flapping erratically around the aviary and refusing to settle for more than a few seconds, and at such times extending her wings for flight, thwarting any effort to slip the bucket over her head. A full-size wheelie-bin would have been more suitable. Repeated attempts to contain her did nothing to improve her untortoise-like temperament. Close confinement within striking distance of an irate and highly volatile female snowy owl is an experience not to be recommended. Even

Trevor, normally unruffled, began to display a modicum of concern, ducking and weaving – outside the pen – in a suitably agitated manner at each near miss of talon and bucket. Eventually, following a wild circumnavigation of the aviary, the owl inadvertently flopped down beside me with wings arched, beak agape and panting with effort. Encouraged by Trevor, with no thought of self-preservation, I dropped the bucket, executed a suicidal dive for both wings, snatched her up and popped her deftly into the box, the operation completed in a trice. With the box lid slammed shut before she realised what was happening, even Trevor breathed a monumental sigh of relief.

Without further mishap the pair were transported – hissing and booing disapprovingly – to their brand new quarters, where, after a few exploratory flights, a spell of trampolining off the netting and a thorough examination of their surroundings, they seemed to settle down quite happily within the space of a few days. Curiously, the birds then began to display a distinct aversion to one another, the far more timid and submissive male, in times of stress, retiring to the far corner behind a conveniently sited log, while the female assumed tenancy of the rest of the aviary.

Observing frequently from my study window overlooking their quarters, I soon realised that the compatibility of husband and wife left something to be desired. The female, by virtue of greater strength and size, obviously wore the trousers, ruling the roost with an iron hand and seeming to regard her much smaller betrothed as lower class and well beneath her dignity. Seldom allowing his tentative attempts to perch beside her to pass unchallenged, she displaced him continually until he was forced to return to his allotted niche in the corner. At feeding times, after a careful look around, the male tentatively emerged to sneak a talonful of chicks and retired sheepishly to his elected corner, devouring his pickings as fast as possible, before his mate polished off the remainder and swooped down to relieve him of what was left of his.

Unlike previous years, the following winter brought semi-arctic conditions, the first heavy snowfall in mid-January accompanied by a cutting east wind that chilled to the bone, its momentum modelling beautiful natural sculptures of snow and piling it into huge drifts, many feet deep. Our small country roads became virtually impassable for several days except to the farm tractor and my four-wheel drive truck, and, to add to the severity of the situation, there followed a succession of cruel wind frosts, turning everything to ice and freezing the surface of the snow rock-solid.

The garden enclosures and aviaries, situated in an exposed position at the edge of the wide-open hillside, bore the brunt of the drifting snow, the owl enclosure in particular ending several feet deep in the stuff by the time the winds abated. The inmates appeared to revel in the situation, possibly the nearest they had ever experienced to their natural arctic habitat.

The intense cold, however, posed a problem. Each time I fed the birds

The female obviously wore the trousers.

with freshly thawed chicks from the freezer, within minutes the food would be completely frozen again before it could be consumed. Fearing possible dangers arising from the owls consuming frozen meat, I decided the only way to avert any problems was to catch them up and house them temporarily inside the sleeping quarters with their food, until the weather relented.

Boarding up the large entrance hole to the aviary, I cleared the interior of drifted snow, scattering a generous litter of dry wood shavings on the floor, before setting about the task of catching them up. By the time preparations were completed, it was already pitch dark.

Locating two, predominantly white snowy owls on a dark night in the confines of a spacious aviary amongst several feet of drifted snow was clearly not all plain sailing, but with the aid of a torch, I eventually discovered two pairs of angry sulphur eyes glaring back at me from ground level, between a low conifer and a vertical tree-stump perch. Actually getting to grips with the owls was harder, though the male, momentarily dazzled by the torch beam, was secured with a deft snatch that took him by both wings, rendering him totally helpless once elevated above the ground. From this position he was quickly incarcerated, and the shed door slammed tightly shut. One down – one to go.

As I had now come to expect, the female, as befits her gender, proved rather more elusive, continually frustrating all attempts to grab her. By the time I finally had her cornered between a nest box and a stunted pine, she was in a vindictive mood. To add to the difficulties, the torch battery suddenly decided to give up the ghost; directing the dim, pathetically flickering beam full in her eyes had no debilitating effect upon her whatsoever. My fingers were stiff and numb with the cold, and a tentative snatch with the gloved hand seized her by one wing only, failing to administer complete disablement, and allowing the cruel talons to come dangerously into play.

The initial sensation was an excruciating pain in my left wrist, as a talon sank home, amazingly, straight through my thickest hawking glove and backed up with an accompanying vice-like grip, bringing tears to my eyes and a string of unprintable oaths to my lips. Lying spreadeagled in the snow and locked in the stalemate of a mutual embrace, the next course of action was debatable. It was impossible to unlock her talons.

Feeling my wrist beginning to throb alarmingly, and a wet trickle of warm blood inside the glove, I edged cautiously towards the shed door, dragging my reluctant captor as I went, still attached with a grim limpet-like tenacity. She maintained the stranglehold as I lifted her, agonisingly, through the door, closing it as tightly as my trapped arm would allow without completely cutting off the circulation.

With the main objective now achieved, at least half the battle was over. Both owls, complete with my left arm, were now inside the hut, while I, rather less safely, remained outside. The next logical course of action was to extricate my arm.

Following a few minutes of sheer agony, to my utter relief I felt the terrible grip beginning to weaken, the owl finally relaxing the half-nelson on my wrist and allowing us both to drop simultaneously, and gratefully, to the floor. Within five minutes I was in the bathroom, studying a deep gash on my left wrist, reeking pungently of antiseptic cream, and making a mental note never to capture an owl by only one wing again.

Whilst on the subject of pain, it was only shortly afterwards that I received one of the more unusual and rather macabre requests regarding my professional services. The inquiry came by phone.

'Have you any experience with humans?' the caller inquired, somewhat tentatively. 'I'd like a little job carried out – as soon as possible.'

Rather tersely, I informed him that besides being no stranger to the basic components of the human anatomy I had, over the years, acquired a modicum of 'experience' with many aspects of the human race, though how this could be even remotely connected with my profession was, at that particular moment, quite beyond me. Prepared for the usual barrage of crude jokes, I noted that it was only mid-morning. The pubs were barely open, and the caller – virtually word perfect – completely lacked the blurred speech and fits of suppressed giggling that regularly accompany such interruptions. The gentleman, in fact, confirmed that he was deadly serious.

Intrigued, to say the least, though quite taken aback by the gravity of the situation, I politely requested he elucidate me further, my mind's eye beginning to conjure up the bizarre vision of a hearse, complete with retinue of pall-bearers, arriving at the front doorstep with a favoured relative or loved one in urgent need of my attention.

31

It transpired that my potential client, during his travels in a naval career, had ended a drunken, nocturnal orgy in some Far-Eastern tattooist's parlour. Sobering up next morning, he was surprised to find himself the involuntary owner of an indelible ornament running the entire length of his right forearm. However good an idea it had seemed at the time, upon reflection he would like it removed. Ideally – as is apparently correct procedure in the more remote corners of the Far East – he would like the offending skin preserved and framed for his sitting room wall, as a reminder of his rather illustrious, if not abstemious, career.

I searched for a way of politely refusing the job without causing offence. I rarely turn down the offer of work, but this was surely verging upon the ridiculous?

I considered the legal aspect. Surely the laws of the land prohibited the layman from carrying out such intricate surgery on a fellow human being? I could probably be charged with at least actual, if not grievous, bodily harm. At the very least, documentation of some description would be required. Although fully licensed to work on the deceased remains of birds, animals, reptiles and the like, I would surely be skating on very thin ice to practise my indifferent skills with a scalpel on *homo sapiens*. Added to this was my pathetic lack of experience in the science of anaesthesia. Short of hitting him over the head with a mallet, or – evidently much easier – getting him absolutely legless, I had little or no means of preparing my client for such potentially painful surgery.

As if to echo my thoughts, the client cautiously inquired whether the removal of such a moderate area of his epidermis would involve any degree of pain. He was, apparently, a little on the squeamish side.

Provided with an easy way out, I began by outlining the more hazardous aspects of the operation, leaving little to the imagination, and sparing no thought for my patient, who winced audibly from time to time as I really warmed to the subject. Allowing my imagination to run riot, I wound up with an alarming inventory of the various tools that would need to be skilfully employed.

The phone remained ominously quiet.

'Hello ... Hello ... are you still there ... ?' A noticeably pregnant pause preceded the eventual reply, the client's enthusiasm now markedly subdued.

'I think I'd better call you back,' he suggested thoughtfully, 'I didn't realise the procedure was quite so ... so ... er ... complicated.'

Politely thanking him for his interest in my services, and confirming that I would be only too delighted to preserve, mount and frame the skin, if he could get it removed rather less painfully, I left the ball firmly in his court by suggesting he consider a consultation with someone in cosmetic surgery. I never heard from him again.

A slow but welcome thaw began a couple of weeks later. Despite an early spring, the passage of time did little to further an intimate relationship between the betrothed snowy owls. Apart from the exchange of a few hesitant hoots at dawn and dusk during a mild April, there was little to raise hopes of obtaining a chick.

After a pleasantly mild winter the following year, a slight advance was observed, the male displaying far more lustily, though he was put back firmly in his place if his attempts to bestow affection were anything other than strictly vocal. His 'intended' displayed no leanings towards debauchery, her virginity, up to this point, remaining stubbornly and resolutely intact. I could only feel sympathy for the poor little fellow; scorned, degraded, treated with utter contempt and clearly outgunned in size, weight, strength and character when it came to any thoughts of seduction. The deflowering of his mate was not to be accomplished easily.

Time passed. Another season came – and went. In fact it was not until the fourth spring that an amazing transformation took place in the male's behaviour. Suddenly brimming with self-esteem, he dared to display in earnest from the highest perch in the enclosure, taking the unheard-of liberty in an attempt to arouse the maternal instincts of his mate. Somewhat crepuscular in activity, he remained silent during the daylight hours, but even then, moved about the aviary with a new air of self-confidence as if staking out a territory, bathing frequently, and with arched wings and flicking tail, openly flaunting himself in a most alluring manner. This more forceful attitude began to take effect, the female showing a marked response, and at last displaying an interest in his feverish exploits.

One morning as I was feeding them, he swooped to snatch a chick, and, much to my astonishment, offered it to the female. When she condescended to accept the gift, he teased her with it, loath to hand it over until she had pursued him, from perch to perch, around the enclosure, and displaying lustily once the exchange had taken place. At dusk the pair courted in earnest, selecting a display ground on a grassy area at the secluded end of the aviary, where the male, amid much boo-ing and concerted tail-flicking, incited his mate to such fever pitch that she embarked upon a wild, outrageous war dance, prancing hysterically up and down, ripping and tearing great divots from the earth in her talons – a remarkably accurate caricature of son Michael, in his most frustrated mood.

Thereafter, every evening, regular pre-nuptial activities took place, the pair ending each session side by side on the central perch, gazing with rapt attention into one another's eyes. A few evenings later Barbara spotted the now promiscuous pair mating briefly on the displaying ground. Disengaging immediately they were seen, they moved apart. From that moment on, twilight orgies became somewhat more clandestine. Though frequently using binoculars from the study window between discreetly drawn curtains, we never again saw them in the actual act of copulation.

While all voyeuristic vigils failed quite miserably, doing the feed round one morning, I was overjoyed to discover a shallow nesting scrape had been excavated on the aviary floor: a wide, saucer-like depression, which the female guarded from a distance, though pretended to ignore. Completely dismissing efforts to provide her with a ready-made nursery, the owl had steered well clear of the large, open-fronted shelters, choosing instead a wide open space beside the hut.

Two days later there was justification for suspecting the female had produced an egg. She remained firmly ensconced upon the nest; the normal procedure – for owls – is for incubation to begin immediately. Clutches may include up to ten eggs, which means that any resulting chicks will hatch at widely spaced intervals, the first and last youngsters varying quite drastically in age and size. The reason for this is sound, though a trifle harsh, for in such hostile conditions, only the oldest, and therefore fittest, are likely to survive.

In the snowy owl's case, during years of an abundant food supply a large proportion of chicks will survive, whereas in leaner times, with adequate food difficult to procure, the later hatched, smaller and therefore weaker members of the brood will quickly perish, leaving more food available for their stronger siblings. This ensures that even in a lean year at least some youngsters should survive to maturity, instead of the entire brood suffering equally, as would happen if all were of identical size and strength, and able to compete on equal terms for any available food.

Time and again I attempted to confirm that an egg had been produced, choosing brief moments when the female ventured off the nest to feed and stretch her legs. But she continually frustrated all attempts by pelting back to the nest whenever one of us was seen approaching the aviary. Slumping down immovably like a gigantic feathered tea-cosy when we arrived at the aviary, she greeted us with a smug and distinctly self-satisfied expression. Over the following days it became quite a ritual, my efforts thwarted repeatedly, whatever my approach route. Barbara and the children thought it quite hilarious; the slightest click of the door latch, or faintest crunch of a footstep on the gravelled path was enough to send the owl scuttling hot foot back to the nest.

Eventually patience paid off. Giving the latest batch of ducklings an evening feed in the brooder house, I paused to peer hopefully through a convenient crack in the back door, only a couple of metres from the aviary perimeter.

A pile of fresh chicks lay untouched by the entrance gate, and from my vantage point I noticed the female beginning to show signs of agitation, glancing around the garden anxiously and longingly studying the pile of food. She was obviously very hungry. This was my chance.

For fully half an hour, I stood with watering eye pressed firmly against the draughty crack, my patience finally rewarded when, having ensured no-one was in sight, the owl carefully lifted up from the scrape. Rousing her feathers, she skipped across the aviary floor to grab a beakful of chicks. This was exactly what I had been waiting for.

To an outburst of warning hoots from the male, I dashed towards the pen, gaining the wire just seconds before she returned at something approaching maximum velocity. Eyes glowering, wings arched, the owl mantled threateningly over the scrape, her face fiercely contorted with rage and indignation. Between her feet, on the bare earth of the crude nesting scrape, lay three exquisite, highly polished white eggs.

4

PISCATORIAL
PREDICAMENTS

A week after I discovered the three eggs, the female was ensconced even more tightly upon the nest, reverently attended to, hand and foot, by the male, who, despite a heavy involvement in the project, preferred to remain at a respectable distance from his spouse during the preliminary stages of her confinement.

When I entered the pen to carry out the menial tasks of removing oddments of uneaten food, and replenishing the bath with fresh water, my actions were viewed with little more than condescending contempt. Her ladyship looked reasonably harmless as she brooded, remaining completely still, though suspicious eyes followed my every move. She clearly still nursed something of a grudge since my inspection of the nest. However, with the bird in such a relatively benign mood, it seemed an ideal opportunity to check the progress of the clutch. Rather foolishly, I decided to risk a quick peep before retiring.

I should have known better. Even by mid-morning it had become clear that it was going to be one of those days. Earlier in the day I had embarked on the marathon task of skinning a recently thawed pike for mounting, and just reached the perilous stage of dislodging the more stubborn and remote ends of the creature's gill plates, when the phone suddenly jangled into life, directly beside my left ear. A most inopportune moment for such an interruption. With the phone hand exploring judiciously, and wrist-deep amongst massed rows of razor-edged teeth, I was hardly prepared for such disturbance. The high-speed removal of one's hand from the jaws of a partly-frozen 8 kilo (17lb.) pike has very little to recommend it. At the time I was barely aware of the needle-like teeth scoring a neat set of lacerations across the back of my knuckles, but within seconds I felt the warm trickle of blood dripping on the linoleum and anointing the mouthpiece of the phone for good measure.

Answering the call whilst endeavouring to stem the flow with oddments of torn newspaper did little to lighten my disposition as I explained to the potential client the many and various ways in which she could – or could

Her ladyship looked reasonably harmless as she brooded.

not – have her pet canary mounted and cased. Virtually on the brink of collapse from loss of blood, I finally persuaded her to call in later that afternoon to view my work, when the decision upon which of my services most suitably fulfilled her requirements could be taken. Quite innocently, she inquired if there was anything in particular that she should do with the deceased specimen in the meantime. Thoughtfully, I refrained from suggesting she use it as a somewhat bizarre form of suppository!

Pausing briefly from my piscatorial endeavours at lunchtime, it was a relief to note that I had at least stopped bleeding, and to enjoy a breath of fresh air after hours of entombment in an airless workshop with an ever-growing mountain of pike fillets, combining the break with the moderately less salubrious duty of clearing up the owl pen. Seeing the inmates so relaxed only made me more anxious to discover just what they had finally produced. The incubator was already warmed up and running, at that moment finishing off the last of the season's waterfowl eggs. A clutch of red-breasted goose eggs, almost on the point of hatching, would be replaced with the owl eggs, once the goslings had been hatched out and safely transferred to the brooding unit in the orchard.

The decision to artificially incubate and attempt to hand-rear the snowy owl clutch appeared to make good sense. Having been fed almost exclusively on a diet of day-old poultry chicks, in captivity some adults, quite understandably, develop infanticidal tendencies, and fail to differentiate between these succulent morsels and their own newly hatched offspring. Many were the horror stories of such events, even an instance of an adult owl rearing a single youngster to a full ten days old, before whipping off its head and gruesomely cannibalising the carcass. Paradoxically, the hand-rearing of young snowy owls is also fraught with many dangers, particularly during the first few days of life, when the chicks are notoriously difficult to sustain. Even with the experience of rearing several difficult bird species with moderate success, from what I could gather, this latest project was certainly a daunting one, with only minimal chances of success.

But, for the moment, all this was rather immaterial. That particular bridge would need to be crossed, if and when I came to it. The old adage 'Don't count your chickens until they're hatched' rings true in relation to the production of almost any form of livestock. At present, the main concern was to discover whether or not the clutch of eggs had been completed.

Armed with the empty refuse container – a large plastic tray – it seemed quite plausible to gently 'encourage' the female from the nest, to allow its contents to be inspected. All this entailed was to ease her gently upwards – as one did routinely with a broodie bantam on a clutch of duck eggs – and all would be instantly revealed.

The male, until that moment minding his own business at the far end of the pen, barked the customary warning of my approach to the nest, shifting silently and suspiciously to a directly rearwards perch to threaten my nether regions. At first content to keep his distance, following a short mutual debate he flew to the female's side, the pair embarking on an animated chorus of anxious hooting and barking. Due to earlier confrontations, I had at least an inkling of what to expect, but this time the reception committee was rather more than bargained for, previous encounters incomparable to the unfettered wrath of an irate female in the advanced stages of incubation. Advancing carefully towards the nest, I crooned to the female in my most soothing tones to allay her anxiety, holding the tray at a full arms length in front, and planning, somewhat whimsically, to employ it to delicately remove her from the nest.

Upon contact, the reaction was immediate. Her behaviour became distinctly un-bantamlike, and of sufficient vehemence to verify the fact that the displacement of a female snowy owl from her nest of eggs is not a task for those of a timid disposition. With the benefit of hindsight, it can only be recommended as an effective, though somewhat bizarre, form of laxative: a course of action upon which to resort only as a last desperate measure.

Gripped in the throes of something approaching spontaneous combustion, she came at me like an express train, the initial talon strike deftly removing a huge chunk with consummate ease from the plastic tray, clasped quite ridiculously and inadequately before me as a shield. Laying back on her tail to expose the huge, red, blood-swollen brooding patch, she advanced, lashing out dangerously, spitting and screaming defiance. Warming to the task, she set about demolishing my pitifully inadequate shield, reducing it in matter of seconds to little more than a saucer-sized remnant; hardly sufficient protection from an armoury of flailing talons and snapping beak. Rooted to the spot throughout the preliminary baptism of fire, I now deemed it prudent to retreat, trusting she would accept the withdrawal by returning to the nest.

Not a bit of it. Following up her undisputed advantage, with renewed aggression she persisted, pursuing me around the enclosure like a demented she-devil, leaving a trail of shattered plastic in our wake.

Fortunately, from such a precarious position, cries for help succeeded in attracting Barbara's attention. She rushed to the goat shed to procure something suitable to replace the dwindling remains of the plastic tray, now alarmingly reduced to little more than a negligible ten-centimetre square.

During the entire rumpus, the male had not moved from the nesting site. Equally fortuitously, his wife's next on-rush allowed me to sidestep with a matador-like agility, and start to retreat in the general direction of the exit gate. As the sole surviving remnant of plastic was ripped from my fingers, Barbara breathlessly appeared, slipping half a sheet of plywood through the gate to act as a replacement for fending off the deluge of blows still raining in on me. With this eminently more practical barrier preventing further advances, between gallantly fending attacks, I paused briefly to count no less than seven eggs in the nest: snow-white, almost round, and becoming smooth and shiny with incubation.

Emerging a little shame-faced, though miraculously without so much as a scratch to add to the earlier wounds, I collapsed gratefully against the gatepost to review the situation. Barbara's only comment was one of praise. 'She's certainly a good mother,' she observed.

Returning dutifully to the workshop after lunch, a hot, gruelling hour saw the obnoxious task of 'fleshing' the pike – the tiresome and protracted scraping of the skin to remove all traces of fat and flesh – completed. I was just about to pop it into the degreasing solution prior to actual preservation, when my lady with the recently expired canary arrived for a consultation. The self-employed pike skinner is, of necessity, something of a solitary soul at times, at least prior to decontamination. Working literally elbow-deep inside a rapidly decomposing fish on a hot day may be construed an anti-social occupation, the resulting unwholesome accumulation of fish slime, flesh, grease and gut renowned for its tenacity. Despite repeated scrubbing, for days the workshop reeks of a Billingsgate gutting shed during a moderate heatwave, and one's hands, arms and clothes remain suggestive of an ancient fish-monger's armpit.

Liberal use of anti-perspirant, pine disinfectant and Barbara's lily of the valley talcum only combined to further abuse the olfactory senses, and it was with some embarrassment that I received my guest in the airless confines of the showroom. Following a brief display of my artistry in its many and varied forms, I suggested hopefully that we continue our discussion in the garden, escorting her on an extended tour of the aviaries.

Hotly pursued by a persistent three quarters of the Norfolk bluebottle population, and an expectant cat that had caught wind of me from the far end of the village, I endeavoured to remain prudently downwind of my client. It came as a great relief when she left, her late pet Gloster canary safely laid out in the refrigerator.

After a gruelling stint of fish skinning, on the rare occasions when retiring to bed with passionate intent, no sooner has one contemplated converting thought into action than one is joined by Spider the cat, who turns up unfailingly with thoughts of a succulent fish supper. Having honed her claws in anticipatory fashion on the corner of the bed, barely able to contain her excitement, she snuffles around expectantly, her nose doing overtime and whiskers wildly aquiver. Discovering nothing even remotely resembling a fish, Spider suspects you are playing games with her, and have mischievously concealed a dead kipper somewhere amongst the bed linen, for which the search is equally protracted and abortive. Just when one is finally allowed to feel reasonably relaxed, the blasted cat hits you full in the stomach and purrs most entreatingly in your ear. Such diversions are hardly conducive to amorous intent and after an exhaustive game of 'hunt the kipper' is over you are long reconciled to the fact that you weren't really bothered anyway.

Perhaps the worst Spider did for my love life was the time she was the most bizarre of an all-embracing list of refusals of an intimate advance. Not for me the oft quoted and comparatively transparent excuses of 'Too hot!' 'Too cold!', 'Too early!', 'Too late!', 'I've got a headache!', nor even the immortal 'We might wake the children!' One never to be forgotten night I received the ultimate in imaginative excuses – 'Not tonight, dear, we might FRIGHTEN THE CAT!'

But, enough of such deviations. A few days later, with the red-breasted goslings safely hatched and installed under an electric heating lamp in a pen below the apple trees, I considered it high time that the owl eggs were collected. To admit that I was not particularly looking forward to the experience would be something of an understatement. At least, this time I knew I was playing with fire and had a reasonable idea of what to expect; I had a healthy respect for my opposite number.

Suitably armed with my thickest hawking gauntlet, a 5mm steel dustbin lid and a distinct sense of foreboding, I entered the aviary and strode gallantly towards the nest with a well rehearsed display of bravado. Most of this immediately evaporated as the male, obviously having undergone a thorough briefing for just such a situation, took up his customary station to the rear, thus erasing any thoughts of a cowardly last minute retreat. Earlier misgivings were shortly realised, the aviary suddenly becoming a far from healthy place to be, its perimeter closing in claustrophobically, and the situation once again instigating a certain disquietening of my lower bowel.

Thus effectively surrounded, and with my confidence diminished to that of a sitting duck on a fairground rifle range, it was the female's turn to enter the proceedings. This time she needed no encouragement to vacate the nest, the extended dustbin lid having the effect of a red rag to a bull. She came at me in a state of high indignation, an evil-tempered, nightmarish bundle of flailing wings and thrusting feet, the commencement of her attack announced by the harsh, repeated drum-roll of talon on steel. Thankful of the dustbin lid's reassuring strength and thickness, I debated what to do next. I had to somehow get past her to actually reach the eggs.

The problem was quickly solved as she came at me again in a jousting lunge, glancing off the bin lid, and ending the attack with a complete reversal of our positions. Fending her off at arm's length, I gained the nest, collecting the eggs carefully inside my hat. Stage one achieved. There was now just the small matter of escaping.

To all intents and purposes I was now quite effectively cornered, the male joining in the fray and standing faithfully beside his mate, ruffling his feathers importantly, though as yet not coming to actual blows. Luckily he was not of such stern stuff as his spouse. Threatening him with the lid put a more tolerable distance between us, allowing concentrated efforts towards safe negotiation of the female. Edging clear of the corner, I steered her around me with the lid. To my surprise, she loped back to the nest in gigantic strides, settling down on the now vacant scrape in ill-concealed disgruntlement. I had secured the complete clutch, mercifully all intact. Making a swift exit before the larceny was discovered, I thanked my lucky stars that the job had been completed without either party incurring grievous bodily harm.

Having successfully completed the abduction, the eggs were borne reverently to the incubator room before being allowed to cool. Prior to setting, each was checked for signs of fertility; this is done with a powerful torch in a darkened room. The torch is held behind the egg and its beam directed through, thus illuminating the contents inside. Almost round, and comparatively small for so large a bird, being pure white, the eggs were quite readily 'candled', the colourless shell allowing the beam of light to reveal the interior in perfect clarity. On careful inspection, it transpired that the owl's first tentative attempts at lovemaking had been rather hit and miss. Out of the seven, only three were definitely fertile, the more advanced egg containing two dark moving blobs – the heart and the eye – joined together with a jelly-like semi-transparent mass, with a spider-like filigree of delicate blood vessels radiating from the centre – the embryonic owlet at about ten days old. Having been incubated for less time, the development of the other two was slightly less advanced, the youngest only just discernible, at most four days old and as yet little more than the faintest suggestion of developing life. It was difficult to conceive that such a microscopic smudge could miraculously develop into a full blown snowy owl.

Just to be on the safe side, I placed the entire clutch in the incubator, marking each side of the shells with a soft pencil to ensure all could be turned correctly each morning and evening. During the incubation process, all eggs require to be turned at least twice a day. This prevents the contents from settling and possibly adhering to the inside of the shell, arresting development and terminating the embryo's life.

Following a few more days of incubation, the eggs were subjected to a further 'candling', confirming the initial deduction of three fertile eggs and four 'clears'; the latter were removed to prevent them putrefying and emitting harmful gasses which might foul the incubator. With the fertile eggs, the air space at the top of each one appeared to be developing correctly as the egg dried out, which by hatching time would occupy almost one third of the interior. The more advanced egg was beginning to darken inside, an indication that the embryo was developing rapidly. A suspicion of a chick-like object was just visible, kicking around spasmodically inside the shell.

On the estimated 28th day of incubation of the more advanced egg, I spotted the first movement inside the shell since – apart from the air space – it had darkened completely: a slight twitching of the inner membrane that encapsulates the chick and separates it from the air space at the larger end of the egg. Pulsing intermittently, it confirmed that the chick was certainly still alive and on the move at last. The long arduous struggle to emerge from the egg had begun with the chick's all-out assault on the inner membrane, which it needed to penetrate before setting to work on the ac-tual shell. Moistening the interior of the incubator with a fine mist sprayer raised the humidity dramatically, an action which softens the eggshell, and to some extent aids the chick's task of breaking free.

A few hours later the entire egg had completely darkened, a tell-tale sign that the chick had ruptured the inner membrane. I listened, entranced, to the first faint tappings from within as the owlet bent to the task of chip-ping its way to freedom, employing the tiny 'egg tooth' situated on the top of its heavy bill.

Throughout the long night and for most of the following day the tiny owlet tapped relentlessly and instinctively against the inside of the shell, its labours occasionally interrupted when faint cheeping noises emanated from within. It was only after many hours of unceasing toil that the chick's persistence finally paid off, a tiny fracture appearing in the surface of the shell and the cheeping becoming louder and more insistent. A final spray-ing to further increase the humidity and the egg was replaced on the mesh of the incubator tray, its progress monitored anxiously through the glass top each time I passed the room. I was greatly relieved when it eventually be-gan to score a line away from the initial fracture, the objective being to sever a line completely around the larger end of the egg, allowing the top to be hinged off like a lid, the trapdoor through which it would enter the great outside world.

The chick's rate of progress at this stage is of paramount importance. It grows so fast that if it took too long to extricate itself the shell would barely allow it to revolve completely around the egg to sever the lid from the inside. The chick could then die trapped, or at best, finally hatch crippled for life. During the course of rearing waterfowl, I had rescued many an emerging hatchling by carefully assisting its work, but the timing of any interference is critical. Intervening too early will cause a premature hatch, with little or not time to allow the adjoining yolk sac to be carefully absorbed by the chick. Too late, and a bird trapped in the shell hatches crippled. Clearly, any attempts to assist the tiny creature's struggle needed timing to perfection.

Monitoring progress through the glass lid with much of the anxiety of an old mother hen, I was relieved when the chick's perseverance was rewarded,

The owlets' overall appearance left much to be desired.

the top section of the shell hinging off to allow what could only be described as a rather grotesque, gargoyle of a head to pop out from beneath a minuscule wing; a tiny, feeble, blind, wobbling head, its eyes tightly closed and the miniature hooked beak emitting faint 'peeping' noises.

Over the years, I have observed many hundreds of eggs in the process of hatching, but such is the miracle that one can never tire of watching. This time I felt especially privileged to witness such an auspicious event, watching spellbound for over an hour as the owlet, in between short rests to summon up reserves of energy, pushed convulsively against the inside of the shell, its emergence unhurried but relentless, until, with a final thrust of its legs, it heaved completely free of the shell, its minute wings and legs clawing ineffectually at the air. Unable to believe its labours had been rewarded, the hatchling expended much time and effort pushing and shoving as if still in the shell, its struggles perambulating it around the interior of the incubator like a tiny tortoise with its tail on fire.

Presently it relented and lay still on the tray, a frail and completely helpless scrap of life, wet and bedraggled and by now suffering the effects of total fatigue. Opening the lid, I gently picked it up for a closer inspection.

The chick felt moist and warm to the touch, the first sparse covering of down still damp and matted. Barely covering my palm, it was unable to lift the proportionately huge head clear of my hand, appearing totally spent and exhausted. The owlet's overall appearance left much to be desired, the scrawny creature totally lacking in grace, and bearing a distinct resemblance to a miniature tennis ball with legs. Feebly it stretched its tiny legs and wings to their fullest extent, the former equipped with fully formed talons, perfect miniature replicas of the adult bird.

Noting the yolk sac had been fully absorbed, I returned the owlet to the warmth to complete the drying process, its thick, eider-down soft covering of velvety-white transforming it before my very eyes into something infinitely more presentable. The tiny egg tooth situated at the end of the curved upper mandible was still intact, an incredible little tool that would shrivel and drop off within a few hours of the chick's emergence from the shell.

For at least the first twenty-four hours the newly hatched owlet would require no feeding, still sustained by the yolk sac inside it, and able to take advantage of the respite to rest and recuperate from its labours. For the first feed, I cut up a day-old chick into minute slivers, crushing the soft bones until the resulting unappetising mess seemed palatably soft and digestible. Using a pair of fine-pointed taxidermy tweezers, I enticed the owlet to peck at offerings of food by rubbing each piece gently against the side of its beak. Although a few tiny portions were accepted and laboriously gulped down, its feeble cries soon ceased, settling down again to sleep and digest the meal when placed in the warmth of the brooder.

Throughout the day I offered food at regular four-hourly intervals; its responses varied, though usually a titbit or two was taken before the chick resumed its slumbers. For some time, all appeared to be going well, but at the end of the third day, I noticed that, although a respectable amount of food was imbibed at the front end, in proportion, relatively little waste matter was appearing at the rear. As a consequence, the owlet's body appeared to be slowly, but surely, swelling. Massaging the vent with a moist pad of cotton wool – a trick that often works with a variety of creatures – did nothing to alleviate the problem, and soon the owlet's body was so tight and distended that it had assumed the gracelessness, portability and unshapely proportions of a water-filled balloon, eventually losing all sense of balance and spending most of the time on its back, pedalling away furiously at the air like an inverted tortoise, a posture most unbecoming and one that boded ill for its future survival. Quite obviously, all was not well.

In desperation, I spent most of the following morning on the phone, contacting various zoos and wildlife parks around the country where snowy owls were kept. Without exception, none offered any real advice, for although a host of other species had been reared with ease, all were united in agreement that the snowy owl was a vastly different proposition. In fact, the nearest I could get to any one hand-rearing a snowy was one that had survived to six days old but eventually succumbed. There was no comfort in the fact that it had displayed identical symptoms to those currently afflicting my owlet.

Despite intensive care and sustained efforts to keep it alive, my worst fears were realised when, as expected, the owlet finally expired at five days old. In the meantime, the second egg had hatched, the resulting chick following an identical routine to its sibling, though this time lasting only three days before succumbing. The final egg showed no sign of even hatching. When later dissected, a fully formed chick was discovered, dead in the shell.

And that was that. My first attempt at rearing a snowy owl chick had ended in absolute disaster. What was possibly worse, I had gained little knowledge as to the cause of the youngster's demise.

The following spring, the adult owls once again went through a strenuous mating routine, the union resulting in a clutch of five eggs laid during late May. Luckily this time, Trevor, the owls' original owner, came to the rescue. It transpired that one of his many contacts in the bird world, Tony, had gained the reputation of possessing something like green fingers regarding the rearing of owls, and had devised a method of hand-rearing snowies during the course of his work at a wildlife park where many species were bred regularly in captivity.

A brief phone call, and, much to my relief, Tony kindly agreed to do his best, though could obviously provide no guarantee of the success or otherwise of the venture. I was only too willing to pass the buck – or in this case the eggs – dreading a re-enactment of the previous year's disaster.

With arrangements finalised regarding delivery, I prepared a suitable container for transporting the eggs. Placing a hot water bottle at the bottom of a large cardboard box, I covered it with a few inches of wood shavings until arriving at a suitable temperature in which to place the eggs during the journey, hopefully without hardboiling them.

By now a fully fledged and reasonably accomplished owl nest robber, I once more took up my trusty dustbin lid and entered the pen. Fully aware of my intentions, my old opponent was soon hooting and barking threateningly, her cries summoning the male from the hut as I displaced her from the nest, to the accompaniment of a deafening and inharmonious rendition on the dustbin lid as she retaliated with flailing talons. Despite the noise, the operation went according to plan until the male, bolder than ever before, flew to attack at head height. With my attention momentarily diverted, the female took advantage. Negotiating the dustbin lid, she snatched an egg in her talons, the terrible grip squashing it like a damp marshmallow. Deft and furious welding of the lid forced her to retreat. Scooping up the remainder of the clutch, I noted with frustration that the squashed egg had been definitely fertile, the network of broken blood vessels plainly visible. Backing cautiously to the gate with the lid extended as a shield, I left hurriedly before incurring further damage.

Candling the remaining four eggs, I was relieved to discover three fertile. Placing them gently among the wood shavings, I set out on the journey, arriving some two hours later and entrusting them to the capable care of Tony. In due course he rang to say that although one chick had died in the shell, the other two had hatched successfully and were doing well, by now hopefully off the danger list and past the most critical stage of rearing. I arranged to collect them a few days later.

Thus it was that Barbara and I, on a sweltering day in mid-July, coasted down the long drive that entered Lilford Park, brimming with anticipation.

5

MEETINGS
AND MISHAPS

During the short space of the week following their collection, the owlets appeared to have grown quite considerably in stature, but when stationed somewhat reluctantly on the perching bar of the hawk scales, their actual weight seemed not to have increased proportionately, much of the increase in size attributable to rapid feather development. The staple diet of day-old chicks had been varied with an occasional feast of wild rabbit meat, which they appeared to enjoy immensely, both gaining in the region of a respectable 200 grammes (7oz). Apart from providing the owlets with a constant supply of food, at such an early age there was little else to be done.

When it comes to training, food has to be cut sufficiently to encourage them to come to the hand when hungry; the basic principle of training a bird is to persuade it to return to the glove. For the moment the owlets needed gorging with food to maintain growth and sturdy feather development, thus avoiding the danger of weak points, or 'hunger traces'. These can develop in the bird's flight feathers if it is fed inadequately, at which juncture the feathers are easily fractured at a later date when working in the field.

During this temporary lull in the proceedings, I decided to clear as much taxidermy work as possible, to allow more free time when the owlets reached a trainable age. Despite limiting the time I spent with them, it was enchanting to discover many of the birds' strange little quirks and foibles, as individual characters emerged noticeably with each day that passed. In the not too distant future I would have to decide which bird to keep for the training attempt. I had realised that keeping both was out of the question, for the time involved in looking after and taming them would be prohibitive. With little or nothing to choose between them at such a tender age, I resolved to keep both birds as long as possible until arriving at a firm decision.

After much deliberation the pair were christened. The male 'Spook', for he would ultimately possess almost completely white and ghost-like plumage as a fully fledged adult; continuing the supernatural theme, the female

'Phantom', a handle that appeared to match her character and disposition to a tee.

Each time I entered the mews they came loping towards me, squeaking shrilly, vacating temporary little 'nests' made nightly amongst the deep wood shavings, where they reclined during the heat of the day with their bodies in deliciously cool contact with the concrete floor. Whenever I found time to break from work they were allowed the complete run of the back garden, mainly during late afternoon and early evening, for as the drought continued with a succession of scorching hot days and cloudless skies, the midday temperature was at times unbearable. Within minutes, both would be panting wearily in the oppressive heat, so much hotter than their natural arctic nursery.

Spook and Phantom soon discovered the back garden was an interesting – though occasionally traumatic – place to be, an excursion within its boundaries always providing something of interest, be it of fur, feather or fin. Occasionally, rather more sinister objects invaded its privacy.

As the heatwave continued relentlessly – well over a month had elapsed since the last significant fall of rain – the corn harvest came into full swing. By mid-morning each day, following evaporation of the early morning dew, the surrounding fields of golden grain were being steadily shorn, the countryside reverberating to the monotonous drone of the combine harvester and the rhythmical rattle and thump of the straw baler following hungrily in its wake.

The barley field beside the garden had by now ripened fully, and the owlets were partaking of their daily constitutional late one afternoon, when the combine came roaring along the adjoining headland, imbibing the standing grain in its wide steel jaws and ejecting loose threshed straw in its wake. Totally entranced by a confusion of peacocks, tortoiseshells and an occasional painted lady on the buddleia bush, the owlets appeared not to notice the mechanical beast approaching until it suddenly appeared alongside the house, a huge red and silver monster belching smoke, noise, dust and straw as it accelerated up the steep gradient beside the garden. At once a remarkable transformation took place. Immediately flattening themselves to the ground in a rather futile attempt to camouflage themselves as a pair of fluffy cow-pats, the owlets presented an almost invisible profile, eyes narrowed to mere slits and woolly heads swivelling in unison to keep the lumbering leviathan under close surveillance. Once safely out of sight over the brow of the hill, both birds visibly relaxed and continued their inspection of the garden.

The inquisitive pair had by now, during the course of regular excursions, been introduced to most of the family, both human and livestock. They had immediately made the acquaintance of daughter Jennifer and son Michael, Whisper the pointer and Muttley the mongrel, the former of whom absolutely doted upon them, including them in garden games as if they were

The inquisitive pair came to rest beside the reclining feline.

two animated cuddly toys. The very last thing I wanted was to 'humanise' the owlets so that they ended up as little more than ostentatious pets, but with both children considerably experienced with a wide variety of birds and animals – and more importantly – reasonably aware of how to treat them, it seemed the experience could be to the advantage of all concerned: educational to the children and helping to accustom the owlets to handling. If they could put up with Michael's unorthodox behaviour, they could withstand virtually anything.

The canine duo remained far less impressionable, wisely preferring the pleasure of their own company, and allowing the potentially dangerous creatures a comfortably wide berth at all times. Spider the cat was definitely less than enamoured with the initial introduction. The lazy feline was discovered one afternoon in the course of their travels, as usual relaxing luxuriously in the sun on a couch of flattened heather, as the daily inspection of the shrubbery got under way. The owlets eventually came to rest – as was their habit at each new point of interest – beside the reclining feline. Her discovery provoked much silent rumination and debate, until the cat stretched a tired leg towards them, an action that prompted an alarmed outbreak of beak-clapping and erratic head-bobbing. It seemed the thing was alive.

At the sound, Spider reluctantly opened a sleepy eye, yawned and stretched lugubriously until her eye focused on the two head-bobbing, goggle-eyed, beak-snapping apparitions bearing down on her; she was then galvanised instantly to life in the manner of proverbial cat on hot bricks. Her tail stuck out and bristling like a bottle brush, with a silent snarl she turned and fled through the bushes, leaving the two explorers – heads still bobbing, eyes wide – peering quizzically into the depths of the shrubbery, clearly pondering why the strange, furry thing had departed in such haste.

Progressing further into the garden, the explorers caused quite a commotion as they inspected the cockatiel aviary, the inmates, with yellow crests erect, protesting shrilly as the two peered in like visitors at the zoo. The Bourke's parakeets, normally quiet and inoffensive, but now guarding four fluffy youngsters in their nest box, added anxiously to the chorus of warning shrieks and scoldings. The lutino lovebirds went completely berserk. In complete contrast, reaching the far end of the aviaries, the Gloster canaries viewed their visit with apparent interest, alighting on the ground and hopping to within a few inches of the owls, tweeting impassively, as the unlikely foursome carried out a thorough and prolonged mutual examination of one another.

Eventually tiring of this, Phantom, possibly the more adventurous of the two, now chose to display her limited skills at mountaineering, scrambling resolutely up the steep face of the nearby rockery. After a few minor tumbles that left her flat on her face, she achieved the topmost pinnacle, a weathered sandstone upon which she paused proudly to take in the surrounding view.

With a second brood of well grown youngsters below the roof eaves, the resident house martins were quick to spot her, dive-bombing into the attack though passing several centimetres above her head. Phantom ducked and weaved in a most agitated manner each time one whizzed perilously close, until one of the martins, much bolder than the rest, came in for a series of low-level sorties, making repeated passes back and forth only millimetres above her head. Phantom's eyes followed it closely, on each dive revolving her head sharply to keep the bird in view. Alas, following a particularly daredevil attack, she leaned too far backwards, and, being rather top-heavy, overbalanced, losing her footing on the smooth stone and executing an untidy reverse somersault. Rolling somewhat ignominiously, tail over tip, the corpulent bundle of fluff and flailing wings came to rest in an indecorous heap of embarrassment on the grass, beak-clapping in exasperation.

Equilibrium fully restored, next on the agenda was the fishpond. Dismissing the concrete frog with the contempt it deserved, Spook ventured to the very edge of the water, spending some time studying the ghostly reflection at his feet, a strange apparition that played hide and seek and glared back at him from the green depths with unblinking eye. Diverting his attention from time to time, one of the large metallic carp cruised lazily around the flowering lilies, or an orange and white veil-tailed comet shimmered tantalisingly past.

And so on, via some remarkably accurate orienteering, to the buddleia bush, where, from the science and fascination of entomology, their studies progressed to herpetology, the transfer prompted by the timely appearance of the large, wart-encrusted toad from beneath a garden edging slab, its progress followed and monitored minutely until it found welcome refuge among the boulders of the rockery. So ended another eventful tour of the garden.

The very next day saw a welcome break in the drought. A cool, refreshing shower of only a few minutes' duration left the land smelling clean and fresh with the scent of wet vegetation, the sweetness of which comes only after the first rainfall following a prolonged period of drought. Despite Barbara's untiring efforts, many shrubs wilted in the garden, the entire back lawn turning sere and dry. Attempting to restore some semblance of greenness, we had resorted to a hose-pipe and sprinkler, moving it around periodically as each area in turn was treated to a thorough, though largely ineffectual soaking. As I moved the sprinkler for at least the tenth time that afternoon, the hose slithered in a snake-like motion past Phantom who, amid the customary hysterical beak-clapping, puffed herself up to twice her normal size, fanned her wings above her head and hissed vehemently, hoping to intimidate the serpent-like creature. Refusing to co-operate, it remained motionless for almost half a minute until, lowering her defences, she back-stepped gradually away from it, almost on tiptoe, with as little loss of face as she could possibly muster.

With an ominously dark cloud drifting overhead to obscure the sun, the first welcome spots of rain fell deliciously on my bare back: huge droplets that sent the dancing butterflies to the underside of leaves, and were absorbed as instantly as ink on blotting paper by the parched ground. Rained upon for the first time in their short lives, the owlets had a fit of hysterics, flapping, prancing and jumping about as if being pursued and stung by a swarm of angry invisible bees, till now ignorant of the strange clinging substance that fell from the sky. Sadly, the shower did not last. Soon the sun was reflecting the colours of the spectrum in countless silver drips that clung precariously to every leaf and flower head, evaporating almost at once in the heat as the owlets, by now steaming gently, roused themselves energetically and shook their plumage dry.

Apart from the dewy coolness of very early morning, the evenings were undoubtedly the most comfortable time of day. Taking advantage of the situation, Barbara served our evening meals outside, the cabaret provided on cue each evening by the incorrigible pair at liberty in the garden. On one such evening, two hot air balloons passed over, rendering both owlets instantly immobile, their combined cowering glare fixed on the huge, slow-moving objects above them, whose progress was followed unwaveringly until safely out of sight, the level of concentration intensified as the flame burners roared periodically to afford them extra lift.

Their old playmate the toad provided another regular diversion, bumbling along unobtrusively beside the patio until he was spotted and followed relentlessly, his acquaintance intimately renewed and subjected to the rudest of scrutiny, until he once more retired to the safety of the alpine garden.

Despite a minor drop in consumption during the hottest days, as my charges grew, their food intake rose accordingly. Quite prodigious amounts were consumed daily, the owlets and their parents now polishing off well over twenty day-old chicks and the best part of a rabbit each day; small wonder indeed that I was kept busy procuring constant supplies of fresh meat. To ensure they were fully gorged, I still offered food thrice daily, also endeavouring to provide as varied a diet as possible to build up stronger and healthier birds. The mainstay was day-old chicks procured from a nearby hatchery, where the cock birds – as future non-producers of eggs – were sexed out and culled immediately after hatching, but these were heavily augmented with fresh wild rabbits, and as many mice as I could capture in a couple of traps set beside the food store in the waterfowl enclosure, a renowned gathering place for both house and wood mice, made doubly attractive by a regular supply of spilled pellets or grain. Swallowed whole in a single gulp, the mice were regarded as nothing more than a tasty titbit, Phantom quite capable of polishing off at least eight at a single sitting.

Rabbits were rather more substantial, but to avoid the dangerous consumption of lead shot by the owlets, needed to be taken by alternative methods to the gun. The use of snares was productive in suitable locations, but on occasions I added to the tally by resorting to a rather neat childhood trick, perfected before I was hardly old enough to be entrusted with a shotgun.

Adjacent to the area where I regularly worked a line of snares, lay an open cattle pasture beside a small copse, where during the summer months the rabbit population had increased to almost plague proportions, the pasture headland laid completely bare where they had nibbled the grass level to the dusty earth. On such open ground, snaring was completely out of the question, and to add to the problem, a small herd of cows also occupied the pasture.

Watching the warren from afar, I noted the three main burrows into which a fair proportion of the rabbits disappeared when disturbed. The next morning, following my dawn inspection of the nearby snares, I blocked each one with a tight wad of twisted hay, cramming it tightly down the holes to arm's length, completely out of sight and effectively creating a dead-end about a metre down the tunnel. Finding themselves unable to navigate the blockage during the day, the rabbits had made their exits via the many concealed 'bolt holes' that always join the warren, which afford an emergency exit in the event of a hunting stoat or such like deciding to investigate the main burrow.

Returning an hour before dusk, the rabbits were feeding well out on the open field. Easily panicked by the sight of me racing towards them, the rabbits bolted immediately for the safety of their burrows, disappearing underground. In the heat of the moment, the blocked holes were forgotten, until they came up against the wad of hay. It was but an easy matter to reach hopefully into each hole and secure an undamaged rabbit or two, helping enormously with the continual headache of supplying fresh meat. Removing the wads of hay immediately afterwards allowed the burrow to be gradually used again, at least until the next food shortage.

Both owlets were invariably at their hungriest in the early morning when, after the comparative coolness of the night, both would beg heartily to be fed; my arrival at the mews would be greeted with much excited shrieking, wing-flapping and insistent pulling at my trouser leg, as, with snapping beaks, they pursued me around the mews like a pair of voracious crocodiles. With scant regard for etiquette or table manners, food was snatched rudely from my fingers and gulped down in as large a quantity as each could muster until, appetites sufficiently dulled, surplus offerings were accepted rather more delicately. Scuttling off to opposite corners of the mews, each concealed its spoils amongst the litter of wood shavings, attempting to look entirely innocent, but casting suspicious glances at the other in case it had been watching. The internment achieved to their satisfaction, they eventually retired to their 'nests', where, replete and contented, they sat in mutual meditation until the pangs of hunger once more motivated further action.

By seven weeks of age, the owlets were progressing literally in leaps and bounds. Spook, the male, though smaller and lighter in weight, was markedly more advanced than his sister, beginning to shed copious amounts of down which was replaced by a sleeker underlay of stubby feathers. Now almost fully grown, his wings were exercised frequently during vigorous workouts within the confines of the garden. At times, a sustained bout of flapping lifted him momentarily above the ground, to which – unable to defy the laws of gravity for more than a few seconds' duration – he would inevitably return with a considerable thump. I became aware of his increasing aviational ability when finding him one morning reposed proudly, if a trifle unsteadily, on the hawk perch in the mews, a point twice his height from the ground to which he certainly could not have climbed.

When outside and pointing ambitiously into any prevailing breeze, a combined hop, skip and jump now carried him the length of the back lawn. In contrast, Phantom preferred to keep both feet firmly planted on terra firma, her progress around the garden restricted to nothing more adventurous than a bumbling, wing-assisted trot, but for all that, she still proved capable of showing a good clean pair of heels when I tried to get her back to the mews, or some equally irksome situation dictated prompt evasive action.

At the climax of the unrelenting heatwave, a day of harsh, cloudless skies and baking sun that sent temperatures soaring well into the nineties, the pair discovered the delights of the garden sprinkler.

The effects of the drought were by now extremely serious and widespread, with crops wilted and flagging in the fields through lack of water, and the garden shrubs and bushes dying despite the frequent watering. Run from our own private water supply, the hosepipe and sprinkler ran full tilt in the early mornings and evenings, when there was less likelihood of evaporation.

Showing some reluctance at first to enter the spray, the owlets stood like a couple of tentative bathers teetering on the very edge of the waves as if afraid of getting their costumes wet, but eventually Spook committed himself and dived bravely under the shower, shaking and flapping his wings in delight as the refreshing jets fell on his back. Reassured by his obvious enjoyment, Phantom followed suit, and soon the pair were revelling lustily in the experience, the droplets running off their backs at first until they roused their feathers, diving in and out of the shower as it played back and forth across the lawn.

After several minutes of such fun and frolics, the bathers had assumed the appearance of a pair of drowned rats, thoroughly drenched, waterlogged and totally bedraggled, in places exposing tiny areas of pink skin. Emerging from the shower suitably refreshed, the owlets appeared to have shrunk to virtually half size, their feathers matted to body contours in a most unflattering manner, but with vigorous preening, rousing and energetic wing-flapping, plumage was soon restored to some sort of order. Following the initial baptism, thereafter on hot days the pair habitually made an immediate beeline for the sprinkler when allowed out of the mews, spending many a happy interval cavorting wildly in and out of the spray.

With confidence growing, daily their explorations became more ambitious, the regular evening rambles taking them gradually further afield and on one occasion ending outside their parents' aviary, their travels monitored and announced along the way as the cockatiels screeched, the canaries tweeted, and a promiscuous hen blackbird, fearing for the safety of her third brood now unsteadily on the wing, swore fluently from the depths of the shrubbery.

The parents' aviary at first appeared deserted, both inmates now heavily in moult and lurking sheepishly in the dark recesses of their hut, where they spent most of the daylight hours during the misery of the moult, sulking bashfully and ashamed to display their temporary shabbiness. Tatty and bedraggled, they appeared furtively at the hut pophole in late evening when all was quiet, venturing out only briefly to feed and bathe. The entire aviary floor was littered liberally with shed feathers looking like the aftermath of a pillow fight.

The owlets' continual squeakings summoned their parents to investigate. The female was first to put in an obviously vexed appearance at the pophole, joined soon after by her mate – now a physical and mental shadow of his former self – who at once disappeared to the far corner behind his convenient tree-stump, from behind which he peered out meekly through eyelids narrowed to the faintest of slits.

The female was far less bashful. Launching towards the owlets, she landed with an athletic bounce beside the wire, guarding her domain with a string of threatening hoots and puffing herself up to assume her most dramatic and intimidating posture, the action dwarfing her offspring as she fixed an evil eye upon the creatures that had dared to disturb her afternoon nap.

Relatively undaunted, after a backward step or two, Spook and Phantom returned her stare, the pair head-bobbing in unison as 'mother' was scrutinised in some considerable detail. Their complete indifference to her threats seemed to have an unnerving effect on the female, who, after taking off and completing three mad circuits of the aviary, clouted full tilt into the wire. Bouncing off the fence, with dazed expression she picked herself up, rather groggily took to her wings and disappeared in a huff through the pop-hole to hoot, hiss and boo in extreme annoyance. She was obviously quite put out.

A similar state of disquiet seemed to accompany the owlets wherever they went, particularly amongst the local birdlife, which seldom passed up the opportunity – as is their habit – of mobbing any owl unfortunate enough to be discovered abroad in full daylight and, as the local tawnies would undoubtedly testify, hounding them relentlessly upon any deviation from their clandestine nocturnal activities.

Accompanying me for the first time on something of a nature ramble, Spook and Phantom caused quite a commotion as they travelled conspicuously along the lane that runs beside west lake: a wide expanse of water covering many acres, left in the aftermath of years of gravel extraction from the wide river valley.

Progressing slowly along, a string of obscenities emanated from every bush and nettlebed, as whitethroats and buntings swore unashamedly at the owlets, one brave soul hopping to within a few feet of where they stood, totally unrepentant, until it glimpsed me close by and retreated to its secret, twilight world of shady bushes. A great tit wheezed a warning from a tall ash, black-headed gulls swirled overhead screaming in annoyance, and blackbirds, tails flirting cantankerously, chortled away in alarm along the desiccated hedgerow.

Consequences of the prolonged drought were much in evidence, the dehydration prompting a premature autumn along the adjoining hedgerow, where trees, starved of life-giving moisture, already hung tarnished with browning leaves. The undergrowth of bramble bushes was wilting visibly, the thorny sprays of fruit still green but shrivelling, and the crop of purple sloes on the blackthorn, hardly bigger than damson stones, had dried and wrinkled to resemble miniature prunes. Even the hawthorn scrub, normally by early August weighed down with a bumper crop of blood-red haws, held instead a sparse sample of dead and browning berries, many of which had already fallen to the ground amongst clumps of brittle bracken that crackled dryly underfoot. Such signs boded ill for the hordes of winter migrants, soon to arrive on our shores, their crucial winter fare already in pitifully short supply.

In complete contrast, the wildflowers seemed to be revelling in the heat. In only a tiny section of the hedge I counted at least a dozen species in full flower, among them the purple stencil brushes of knapweed, pink, white and bladder campion, two kinds of willowherb, dwarf mallow, toadflax and a profusion of others, with the vine-like tendrils of cornbine bound inextricably among the vegetation supporting a mass of blushing flowers, their brightness much enhanced by the colourless backcloth of decay.

Oozing devilment, the wicked two-some accompanied me in fits and starts down the lane, their progress interrupted at each new sight and sound, displaying an interest in everything from a scrap of silver paper twinkling in the grass to the many creatures that hopped, flew or fled before them down the lane. A host of butterflies and grasshoppers were disturbed at every forward step, among them a profusion of wall browns in easily distinguished pairs that flirted shamelessly prior to mating. The females, larger in size and lacking the dark diagonal wingbar of the males, alighted on the bare

A string of obscenities emanated from every bush and nettlebed.

earth to flutter their wings seductively to their attentive partners, the pair joining together and taking wing in tandem to flutter rather more laboriously down the lane.

Spook, completely captivated by the sex life of the wall brown, stood entranced, the furthering of his knowledge in all things carnal interrupted, as the inseparable pair at his feet prudently took wing over the hedge to continue their orgy in private. The spell broken, he trotted off to examine the cumbersome movements of a large bumble bee, bumbling clumsily from flower to flower on the ubiquitous knapweed, droning drowsily as it carried out its toil.

Here he was joined by Phantom, equally interested until a wedge of greylags, cackling loudly, took off from the lake, their flightpath bringing them directly overhead, a clamouring squadron skimming the hedge in vee formation, bound for the shorn stubble at the far end of the valley where the harvest was good. Aware of their approach, the owlets crouched fearfully amongst the brittle grass stems, and in view of their colouring blended surprisingly well into the background as they crouched, completely still, not relaxing until the geese had swept safely out of sight over the nearby marsh.

The limit of our excursion was the small carp pool at the bottom of the lane; a kingfisher exploded like a neon bullet from a dead branch overhanging the pool, its waters green and murky with summer algae, above which a riot of azure damselflies glinted metallically around the margins of reed mace. A distantly related cousin, the brown aeshna, propelled itself swiftly across the water on transparent wings of gauze, coming to rest on a flower-studded clump of lily pads, around which the great dorsal fins of corpulent mirror carp cleaved the surface as they cruised lazily round and round, their scales reflecting like polished pennies in the sunlight.

For fully half an hour we sunbathed on the steep bank of the sheltered pool, the owlets tired and drowsy after their exertions and apparently content to merely sit, watch and listen to the sleepy purr of a turtle-dove in the bankside willows, the cries of terns fishing the causeway shallows and the exuberant flutings of an oystercatcher in stiff-winged flight disturbed from its island retreat, as the first thistledown seeds of the rosebay willow-herb spikes drifted lazily past on a warm sigh of air.

But all good things must come to an end. Our dozings were shattered as the gravel cart, its engine at full roar, came rattling along the causeway with a consignment of sand, putting to flight a blizzard of protesting gulls and trailing a choking smokescreen of dust in its wake. A willow warbler, its needle-like beak brimming with insects for its clutch of tiny young, hissed annoyance from the safety of the marginal sedges as we began the slow trek home.

6

A FOX IN
THE FOUNDATIONS

The kindly, but unfamiliar, voice on the phone informed me that, following a harrowing and protracted illness, 'poor old Billy', had at long last passed peacefully away. I racked my brains: who on earth was Billy?

A mumbled, but suitably sympathetic, 'I'm terribly sorry to hear that,' appeared to cover most of the immediate possibilities, as I awaited a hint of who, or indeed what, we were actually discussing.

Was there the possibility of a long-lost uncle, cousin, in-law – even outlaw – several times removed, leaving me a little something in his will? Or, more likely, was the call a gentle hint that I was expected to fork out for some kind of wreath to mark poor Billy's passing?

Luckily, nothing quite so drastic, as the lady with the deep, lilting Irish brogue soon convinced me that the call was to me in my professional capacity.

'Of course, we had been expecting it to happen for some time,' the sorrowful voice related, ' ... though it's still a great shock. His poor wife is absolutely heartbroken and pining dreadfully. She looks so lonely and pitiful, all on her own in that big cage.'

At the first mention of 'cage', I now felt reasonably confident the assumption was correct. Short of being unspeakably hen-pecked, the single fact that Billy had formerly resided therein at least narrowed the field quite considerably. All sorts of weird and wonderful creatures are kept in cages.

A parrot? Dwarf rabbit? A Russian hamster? A chinchilla? Lions and tigers also live in cages, but this was obviously a pet, and, by the sound of it, much-loved.

I have always been wary of, and often decline to work on, intimate family pets, especially most types of larger mammal. Dogs and cats are definitely a no-go area as far as I am concerned, for, as I repeatedly try to impress upon potential clients, however skilfully a preservation job is carried out, there is just no way – apart from pure luck – that any taxidermist can hope to recapture the exact essence of expression of an animal that its owner has come to know and love. At best, the most professionally competent mount can only be a mawkish, heart-rending reminder of the former bright-eyed and bushy-tailed animal. Far better to make a clean break, replace it with a living animal, and preserve only happy memories of a much-loved pet.

This fact was strongly emphasised by my original tutor, Fred, who on one occasion painstakingly preserved an adored household tabby for an elderly female client, only to be told upon collection that it was definitely not her cat, the irate lady demanding in no uncertain terms to know just what he had done with the real one, and why he was trying to palm her off with such an inferior substitute. The ultimate outcome was bad feeling on both sides. The client stormed away cat-less, leaving Fred unpaid and the unfortunate feline to end its days as an unconventional, though highly effective scarecrow in the vegetable garden.

Billy, in fact, turned out to be a budgerigar, a pale cobalt creature with a massive stomach growth to which, despite regular veterinary consultations, he had at last inevitably succumbed. Through no fault of his own, Billy epitomised just about everything that the self-respecting taxidermist dreads. A budgie with a tumour the size of a golf ball is no longer a thing of beauty, and this one in particular had assumed the obese proportions of a winged Penfold Ace. It would be sensible to decline the job.

Seeing the dear lady's distress at such a suggestion, much against my better judgement, I felt obliged at least to try to preserve it for her, preparing the workbench and tools to make a start immediately she had left.

Groaning inwardly, I set to work. Skinning carefully around the tumour, I attempted to remove the tissue-like skin, which would then allow a rough evaluation of what problems lay ahead. Blood and cloying slime from the disturbed tumour adhered to the body feathers in roughly equal and profuse quantities, but with the skin safely removed, I could at least begin the delicate cleaning process. For the rest of the day I retired to the workshop, attempting to remove the very last spot of blood and stubborn smear of dirt and slime, soaking, cleaning, drying, soaking, cleaning, drying, with what seemed like endless monotony. It was only after several stressful hours of painstakingly preening each feather into place, that the skin looked of a sufficiently pristine quality to grace the cover of a seed packet.

But this was only half the job. Immersing the skin overnight prevented it from drying out and becoming unworkable, while I gained a few hours' respite before the final blow-drying and mounting the skin over an artificial body. In fact, the job occupied the best part of a frustrating morning, before I was satisfied it was up to scratch. Sewing minor tears in the skin, carefully wiring out and re-modelling each tiny limb precisely, and finally mounting and binding the plumage in place prior to drying out. The result looked quite encouraging, though cost me dearly in time, patience, and several degrees of blood pressure.

In restoring this single tiny bird to an acceptable standard, I had invested as much time as it would have taken to preserve and mount at least a couple of normal specimens, but could charge very little for the end result. The client, quite logically, though unfairly, expects to be charged a price directly relevant to the size of the job, no matter the difficulty involved. Not versed in the mechanics of taxidermy, most people fail to grasp that the entire pains-taking, tedious and extremely time-consuming procedure is the same whatever the size of the specimen involved, be it wren or peacock, redstart or pelican. Small specimens are notoriously difficult to work on, and far more easily damaged, but something a tenth the size of a pheasant is ex-pected to cost a tenth of the price, and it is seldom possible to charge anything appropriate to the work involved.

Having at least the satisfaction of a job well done, I had earned a little free time with the owlets.

Exactly three weeks had elapsed since their arrival, and now, although their heads still remained clothed with a generous balaclava of fluffy down, most of the coarser grey body down had been shed with the appearance of their juvenile plumage. Almost two thirds covered with feath-ers, in consequence the owlets were looking far more elegant and refined, with developing wings and tails lending length to sleeker body lines, now resembling the rather more aerodynamic contours of their parents. The dif-ference was amazing, compared to the tatty and moth-eaten accumulations of fluff, feet, beaks and eyes I had collected only three weeks previously.

When not indulging in their two favourite pastimes of feeding and sleep-ing, the owlets spent more and more time in frenetic wing-flapping, the regular exercise beginning to build up and strengthen developing pectoral muscles in preparation for flight. That the owlets were capable of flight was now beyond question, though as yet they lacked the muscle and stamina for sustained aviation. Spook, considerably more advanced in aeronautical studies, had certainly discovered an easier way to circumnavigate the garden, his frenzied flappings conveying him rather unsteadily from patio chair to table top, from table top to garden swing, from swing to pumphouse, and so on to the rockery, with Phantom, markedly less adventurous, puffing behind like a broken-winded donkey. Unable to keep up with his wild per-ambulations, she as yet lacked the ambition of her brother, whose take-offs and flights improved spectacularly with each day that passed.

When Phantom finally threw caution to the winds and took to the air, the flight was short. Covering the first few yards quite competently, she passed the end of the house, where a vicious crosswind caught her squarely amid-ships, sending her erratically off course. With no time to lower her landing gear, she crash landed in a nearby berberis bush from where, spread-eagled uncomfortably across its boughs, she had to be slowly and painfully extricated with due respect for the thorns.

With the owlets becoming fully, if rather unsteadily, airborne, their movements would soon need to be restricted, or at the very least, monitored rather more carefully. I still awaited delivery of their 'furniture': the accoutrements of falconry. The 'jesses' – made to measure leg straps crafted from very fine leather – would afford some control over their movements and, with swivel and leash attached, allow the birds to be tethered to a weathering block in the garden with no fear of them wandering. Until the equipment arrived, extreme vigilance needed to be exercised.

The same level of attention should have been given to the pen of red-breasted goslings in the orchard next morning. The birds effected a mass breakout at feeding time when, having moved their pen to a fresh area of grass, I dished out the morning ration of pellets. In a hurry as usual, I took the water fountain to the rear of the mews for refilling, in my haste neglecting to close the pen door securely. Once engrossed in feeding, the goslings normally had no intention of straying, but with a slight gust of wind the door swung open on a broken hinge. Bursting out simultaneously, with room to stretch their wings at last, they ran and flapped hysterically in all directions, scattering to the extremities of the garden and disappearing without trace amongst the undergrowth, leaving me wondering where to start searching. The goslings, eight in all, nearly full-grown and each worth the best part of what I laughingly call a week's wages, had become imprinted on me at an early age. Finding not so much as a feather on an initial desperate search of the garden, I decided to put its powers to the test.

Walking, as calmly as the situation allowed, around the perimeter fence, I repeated my usual goose-like whistle of greeting.

As if by magic, one by one the goslings emerged from hiding, and by the third complete circuit of the garden I was delighted to count all eight trailing happily behind me, a strung-out crocodile of cackling goslings following dutifully in my wake. The flock fully mustered, with the expertise of the Pied Piper of Hamlyn, I led them confidently back to their quarters. With the first one safely through the door, the rest quickly followed, having thoroughly enjoyed a spot of early morning exercise in the garden. Breathing a deep sigh of relief, once again I was left to marvel upon the extraordinary powers of imprinting.

Shortly afterwards, while receiving an early customer in the showroom, I was pleased to note that Billy the budgie appeared to be drying out quite nicely, and would soon be ready to receive the finishing touches. The customer had discovered a dead vixen on the road during the night, bringing it round for rough quote and evaluation.

Apart from the obviously fatal argument with a motor vehicle, the animal was in the pink of health and condition. As Barbara peered quietly around the door to inform me of a phone call, my client was experiencing some difficulty in explaining the finer points of the exact pose in which he desired the finished mount, finally resorting to a charade of crouching on all fours beside my desk. Squatting low, head cocked attentively, muscles tensed, he was poised as if to spring at some imaginary prey, supposedly lurking in the region of the waste paper basket.

Unable to recognise the very picture of vulpine alertness, a look of total incredulity crossed Barbara's face as she attempted to discover just what on earth I was doing with my latest customer. Thanking my lucky stars it was a male client, I supressed a fit of the giggles with some difficulty, gratefully excusing myself and following her quickly out of the door.

'It's your "budgie" lady again,' Barbara explained, 'she still seems quite upset.'

Handing over the phone, Barbara said she would return to keep an eye on my early morning client, until I had dealt with the call.

'Don't worry,' I replied, 'I'm sure he won't touch anything.'

'I wasn't worried about him making off with one of your prize specimens,' she quipped, 'I was more concerned he might pee up the leg of the snooker table ...'

I bid good morning to the still tearful Irish voice, explaining that I had restored Billy to the best of my ability, though suggesting at the same time if she shouldn't have got over the shock of losing him by now.

'It's not poor Billy that I'm so upset about,' she sobbed woefully, ' ... it's his mate. She's just died of a broken heart.'

It was now my turn to almost burst into tears, as I awaited the inevitable request.

'Can you preserve her, so I can always keep them together?'

Extreme sympathy and sorrow were most sincerely felt. My Irish lady wasn't the only one in deep mourning as I confirmed that I would be ready to receive her shortly.

The owlets provided more light-hearted entertainment. They now knew the garden pretty well, so on their next outing they were more adventurous, venturing over the kitchen threshold one morning much to the consternation of the dogs, both flat out and enjoying a quiet snooze on the dining room floor. Before I could usher the dogs outside, the Chinese evergreen standing innocently at the end of the breakfast bar had gone for a burton, crashing sideways at the merest touch of Phantom's wing as she flapped clumsily across the polished floor, achieving at least a nine point four in performing the snowy owl equivalent of a quite immaculate triple salchow, skidding to a standstill using her talons as brakes. The unseated pot plant spilled compost far and wide, shedding an odd leaf or two, which were added to as Spook exercised his beak by taking a few competent cuttings for good measure.

To avoid any close confrontations, I grabbed both dogs by their collars and dragged them outside, shutting the bottom half of the stable door behind them, but not before Muttley, head down and tail at half mast, had assumed full responsibility for the damage, piddling nervously on the kitchen floor, then standing in it and tramping about to ensure its even distribution.

He was poised as if to spring at some imaginary prey.

By the time both dogs were safely out of the way, Spook had tired of pruning the pot plant and was now involved in an assault on the brand new kitchen mat, tearing out the tassels and flicking them aside, while Phantom, bemused by the clicking of talons on the linoleum, became engrossed in a wild game of hopscotch, her clicketty-clacking across the floor boosted by intermittent bouts of beak-clapping. Luckily Barbara was out for the morning.

Whilst I restored the Chinese evergreen to an upright position and the kitchen floor to its former unsoiled condition, the miscreants again disappeared, bypassing the dining room and arriving in the hall, where they spent a few moments admiring a stuffed barn owl, encased in a glass dome, staring unseeingly back at them with glassy, unblinking eye. Discovering their smaller cousin impossible to outstare, they progressed to the sitting room, where the children – making the very utmost of the long school holiday – were watching television.

Although expressing an initial interest in the moving pictures, they soon tired of the inevitable black and white repeat, and when the adverts interrupted the rather tenuous storyline they immediately lost interest.

Displaying not the slightest curiosity in the revelation of an even whiter washing powder, nor indeed in the merits of the leak-proof nappy, Spook passed a suitable comment by lifting his tail and committing a minor indiscretion on the fireside mat. Not to be outdone, Phantom, by virtue of her greater size and quite prodigious appetite at breakfast time, committed a rather less than minor indiscretion, her action sending me rushing to the bathroom for the toilet roll and a damp cloth. When extensive mopping up operations had been completed, the playful pair were heavily into an evidently thrilling game of musical chairs. Using the furniture with gay abandon, they tested the springiness and trampoline qualities of the three-piece, their wild cavortings spreading a veritable blizzard of wood shavings, waxy feather shafts and copious amounts of down around the room.

Within the space of five minutes, the sitting room was transformed into a disaster area. Swearing the children to secrecy, I got out the hoover. The noise upset the owlets greatly, encouraging even more energetic flapping that served only to send the debris further around the room. I was always one step behind in clearing up the devastation, and at this point it seemed only sensible to return the miscreants to the mews before Barbara's imminent return.

Guiding the birds back to the kitchen, where the floor was at least washable, I finished the hoovering and placed a convenient pot plant over the indelible stain left by Phantom on the fireside mat. The sooner I got them outside the better.

The owlets were obviously of much the same opinion. As I picked up Phantom ready to carry her back to the mews, Spook, tiring of his attempts at origami with the morning press, was already warming up for flight, judging distances, measuring angles, and, before I could stop him, using the kitchen mat as a runway to attain maximum revs and launch towards the top of the stable door.

Greatly overshooting the mark, he disappeared over the top, crash landing on Whisper, reclining peacefully in the sun. The next few moments were of utter pandemonium, and I can only hazard a guess at how the chain of events unfolded, although the evidence of wreckage lay far and quite widely distributed.

Whisper, galvanised into sudden action by Spook's untimely descent on top of her, had bolted like a sprinter out of the starting blocks, colliding with the patio furniture, and sending the table, chairs and umbrella stand in all directions. The umbrella stand inevitably fell on top of poor old Muttley, who let out a mournful wail and vanished. Spider the cat vaulted the stable door without touching it, the cockatiels screeched, the parrots swore, the Hawaiian gander cackled defiantly and the orchard geese went berserk, flapping and running in all directions, crashing into the fences and one another like a flock of headless chickens. Only the border canary remained unruffled, trilling away joyfully without a care in the world.

Reaching the scene of devastation, I discovered Spook perched quite unperturbed on the broken umbrella stand, exploring all about him as if trying to establish the cause of all the fuss. There was no sign of either dog, Whisper probably still running and Muttley laden with guilt for an unprecedented second time within minutes, probably lurking deep in the shrubbery on the verge of tears, a dark cloud of depression hanging ominously above him.

The jesses were desperately needed, for now the owls were beginning to fly they seemed to cause havoc and uproar wherever they went. The household had hardly suffered such damage since the occasion the local midwife had 'delivered' a fox cub – and I use the word advisedly – from the unlikely location of the house foundations: an action that undoubtedly saved the cub's life but almost brought about my premature demise by asphyxiation.

It all started quite innocently enough, when a friend discovered the tiny fox cub wandering aimlessly at the roadside on his early morning paper round. Something of a good Samaritan, he picked it up and deposited it on our doorstep with the morning paper, knowing full well that at the time we ran something of an open house for orphans and strays.

Before finding it a suitable home, the cub was housed temporarily in a passageway adjoining the kitchen, from where, when answering the call of nature, he effectively succeeded in stinking out the entire household, so pungent were his bowel movements when fed on an emergency ration of day-old chicks. The diet seemed to have the most debilitating effect on his digestive system, but apart from this regular olfactory abuse, he was very little trouble to look after and eventually we fixed him up with a suitable home, the potential owner having just lost a vixen that had been a household pet for many years.

Alas, the day before the cub was due to be collected, the kitchen door was inadvertently left ajar. Discovering the passage empty, we immediately instigated a full scale search of the premises, for all doors leading to the garden were firmly shut, and the cub could have gone no further. For twenty minutes we searched in vain; each and every room, all the cupboards, under the bed, below the stairs, in the spare loo and even up the chimney, but there was neither hide nor hair of the missing cub, nor the faintest poignant whiff to betray his hiding place.

Totally stumped, we paused in the sitting room to discuss the situation logically. It appeared the cub had somehow completely vanished into thin air. Debating just where to search next, I stopped Barbara in mid-sentence as a faint rattling and weird snuffling noises came from somewhere below our feet. Dismissing the possibility of a poltergeist, we eventually narrowed the source of the sound to a small area in one corner of the room, the truth beginning to dawn at last. I rushed upstairs to the study and discovered, in the depths of a crawlway cupboard, a fox-cub sized hole in the cobwebs covering an open section of the cavity wall. The four-inch cavity fell sheer to the house foundations, ending a full three feet below ground level.

During the initial hurried inspection, I had not even paused to consider the cub entering such a confined space, but he had literally gone to earth down the cavity, a one-way journey that ended twenty feet below.

What could we do to retrieve him? Short of knocking out the gable end of the house, there seemed few options.

Returning to the sitting room, we could still hear the cub moving around the foundations, the rattling caused by his feet displacing the loose chips of mortar lying in the wall cavity. The only way of establishing some sort of contact was to lever the quarry tiles from the nearest window sill, and with this completed, the torch beam located a mischievous pair of twinkling eyes five feet below the sill, the cub oblivious to the gravity of the situation and whimpering pitifully to be fed.

To lure him closer, Barbara dropped a chick down the cavity, the cub barely able to move towards it along the narrow gap, but after a short struggle we heard him munching hungrily. Not allowing him the opportunity to move again, I rammed a convenient length of three by two timber down each side of him, effectively curtailing further movement.

Setting to work again with the hammer and chisel, I then dismantled a section of the sitting room wall directly towards the cub. On reaching floor level, I found to my dismay that I was still, even at arms length, unable to reach it.

There was only one thing for it. I would have to excavate a trench to the base of the foundations from the outside, then chisel a hole through the exterior brickwork to reach the exact point of the cub's imprisonment.

This I did, eventually knocking a hole through the wall of sufficient size to locate the cub, but at this point I had to cease further demolition work for fear of crushing him in the process. Lying flat on my stomach, I reached down, located the cub's head and carefully eased it out as far as I was able. Although the head came clear, it was obvious that the rest of the body would not follow. I dared not pull any harder for fear of decapitating the wretched creature. Stalemate!

It was at this very moment that the midwife made a timely appearance to examine Barbara: several months pregnant at the time, she seemed at that particular moment in imminent danger of having kittens. In her capacity of midwife-cum-animal rescue service, the nurse quickly sized up the situation, winding me completely by plonking her umpteen corpulent stones across the small of my back.

Reaching down to snatch the cub's head from my grasp, the shift of weight caused an immediate and acute shortage of breath as, in something approaching a semi-conscious stupor I watched, disbelieving and enthralled. With the expertise borne of long experience in midwifery, she delivered the cub like a rabbit out of hat.

Had I not, through a distorted and painful red mist, actually witnessed at first hand the delivery of such a large cub from such a small hole, I would scarcely have believed it possible, but as the midwife later informed me as I sat recovering from the edge of total blackout, she had been in the business of persuading large objects out of small apertures for years.

As my respiration began to improve, the nurse spotted a nasty looking gash on the back of my knuckles, caused by an enthusiastic, though inaccurate swipe of the hammer. It certainly looked deserving of an anti-tetanus shot.

She delivered the cub like a rabbit out of a hat.

Aware of her widespread reputation of having the finesse of a dart player when it came to administering injections, I elected to pass up the experience, but ignoring my protests, she scuttled off to her shooting brake, returning with a wicked-looking syringe already loaded and poised for action. Having gained my second wind, I was long gone before she had even re-entered the house.

The wound – and the fox cub – eventually took a turn for the better. Only the sitting room wall still bears the scars, the repaired brickwork and rough plastering standing out like a sore thumb against the smoothness of the wall. That reminds me – I really must fix that window sill ...!

7

A SHAG
IN THE BATH

Thankfully, at long last the parcel of hawking equipment arrived: a set of soft leather jesses for each bird, two immaculate pairs of shiny brass leg bells and a brace of strong steel swivels, together with leashes of braided nylon for tethering the owlets to their weathering blocks.

I had also treated myself to a new hawking gauntlet crafted from soft deerskin which, not surprisingly, fitted like a glove, its predecessor ruined by the abuse of a succession of birds of prey, not least of all from Spectre, the boisterous buzzard. With all this tackle I should be able to control the owlets completely.

The need of such restraint was clearly obvious the following morning, when I rather foolishly left the mews door ajar while dishing out the morning feed. After a foodless night, normally the youngsters were reluctant to leave my side when food was in the offing, but on this occasion Spook, having snatched and gulped down a single chick, ventured sneakily out of the door. Jumping immediately to the pumphouse roof, he began to survey his distant surroundings with enthusiasm.

As his most ambitious flight to date had covered only a pathetic ten metres or so, I was not unduly bothered, until he lofted nonchalantly into the air for a quick circuit of the lawn. Instead of flopping heavily to earth within seconds, he began to display a skill and confidence hitherto unknown, swerving skilfully to avoid the parakeet aviary and circling the conifer bed with ease. This was hardly the urgent flapping of a novice to remain airborne. This was the competent, totally assured flight of a fully fledged owl: powerful, buoyant and exuding confidence as he swept, alternatively flapping and gliding, around the garden, having somehow made the transition from the rawest recruit to a fully fledged pilot virtually overnight.

I could hardly believe my eyes. Gripped in the throes of fear, panic and frustration, I watched, completely spellbound, as he revelled lustily in his newly discovered powers.

Breaking out of a regular and monotonous circling, accompanied by a wild fit of cackling from the orchard geese, he lifted easily above the perimeter of their pen, swept high over the adjoining conifer belt, and set off determinedly across the open field.

I must admit to experiencing a certain sense of pride as I watched my young owlet, a mere stripling of nine weeks, winging impressively across the stubble, but this euphoric state was short-lived, and evaporated as the speed and determination of Spook's flight carried him swiftly over the hill.

In desperation I called to him, but I might just as well have invited the rooks circling suspiciously overhead to come to hand. If Spook gained the sanctuary of the nearby wood, now an overgrown jungle of summer leaves and virtually impenetrable undergrowth, it would be almost impossible to locate him again.

Racing out of the garden, I was relieved to see a prominent white mark alight on the brow of the hill, his head bobbing visibly against the golden stubble as he deliberated which way to go. Seeming rather lost and confused, he remained on the stubble until I was within a few metres.

Softly repeating the accustomed food-whistle, I approached slowly, talking to him in an effort to calm him, and extending my hand in the pretence of offering a chick. Almost within range, I suddenly noticed again that faraway look in his eye, as he crouched ready to spring. Luckily my headlong dive took him by surprise, a desperate rugby tackle which caught him squarely across the shoulders, effectively winding me.

The relief was overwhelming, but on the way back as I held him tightly against my chest Spook snapped his beak in protest and pedalled furiously as he tried to rake me with his talons. I had learned my lesson. That was definitely the last time he, or even the less aeronautically orientated Phantom, would be allowed outside untethered, until – and indeed, if – they could be fully trained.

Anxious to make at least some headway towards this goal, the following

My headlong dive took him by surprise.

morning was earmarked for jessing the owlets. I had not been looking forward to the operation, for fear of destroying some measure of confidence the birds had shown towards me by manhandling them; I was also reluctant to deal with the more dangerous appendages of an owl, namely the needle-sharp and extremely powerful talons.

As an extra precaution, I intended to bell the owls at the same time, and with this in mind carefully fashioned two sets of soft leather 'bewits' for attaching the bells, using my little finger, conveniently of similar diameter to a snowy owl's leg, as a guide to a comfortable fit.

Bells are not just decorative; they are indispensable when flying a bird free, particularly when it disappears amongst thick woodland, tall crops or rough vegetation – possibly half a kilometre distant – and fails to respond when called. Top-quality hawk bells are audible over incredible distances, and in such a situation a lost bird making the slightest movement of its legs will agitate the bells, thus leading one unerringly to its hiding place.

The relatively straightforward task of attaching jesses to a common or garden hawk is a two-man job: one to hold the bird and prevent it struggling, whilst the other attaches its 'furniture'. With a full-grown snowy owl – as we were soon to discover – another pair of hands would have been helpful.

Spook, sitting calmly on the mews block, was the first to be kitted out. Although normally quite amenable, he objected violently to being picked up and suspended aloft by the base of his wings, his talons scrabbling treacherously at the air, clasping immediately and firmly upon anything with which they collided. The first thing happened to be my left hand. I managed to seize one of the questing feet, but the other got my hand in an agonising grip. I extricated an inside talon from a nasty position at the base of my index finger, but no sooner had I released it than he grabbed again, this time finding my wrist, only marginally more bearable. At least it stopped his struggles and allowed the adjoining hand some freedom of movement to work on his other leg.

The main trouble was that Barbara has relatively small hands, both of which were employed in holding the bird aloft, unable to exercise any restraint at all over the flailing talons. Attempting to keep one leg out of harm's way while working on the other was a virtually impossible, extremely painful and most frustrating exercise.

Gritting my teeth I started work, clipping a few feathers from the long 'trousers' that clothed his legs, and beginning the painstakingly slow process of threading the leather straps back and forth through one another and pulling them tight, the end result being an immovable, though comfortable anklet, culminating in a 25 centimetre (10 in.) strap.

The jess firmly in place, the bell was fixed above it with a leather bewit in a similar manner, to more outbursts of wailing, screeching, spitting and swearing, admittedly not all of it from Spook. The other foot received much the same treatment as before. Having checked everything was firmly fixed and quite comfortable, Barbara replaced Spook on the floor. He immediately pranced off to his favourite corner of the mews, alternately glaring daggers at us and inspecting his new legwear, lifting up each foot in turn and examining it studiously as though fearing he had trodden in something unpleasant.

Phantom was next. Having noted her brother's distress, she seemed fully aware that she was to receive the same treatment as we manoeuvred her into a corner, by now in one of her less than co-operative moods, and immediately assuming the number one owl posture of self defence, lying flat on her back with talons poised, daring anyone to even contemplate picking her up. Eventually Barbara gained a hold, lifting her firmly but gently off the floor and conversing in her sweetest tones while I dealt with the more painful side of things. Of the two owlets, Phantom certainly proved the more difficult to handle, at the very outset succeeding in manacling me by both hands, resulting in an impasse of Barbara holding Phantom by both wings, while she in turn had me effectively handcuffed with a wrist clenched in each of her talons. That way we were unlikely to make a great deal of progress.

It was to get even more complicated. Suffice it to say that by the time we had finished, I had long since become immune to pain. When we completed the final fitting, we released Phantom with an enormous sigh of relief, and I went off to lick my wounds and allow the birds to accustom themselves to their new outfits. Luckily, Barbara had escaped with hardly a scratch, but during the engagement I had acquired several lavish gouges from the elbow downwards. These I immersed in disinfectant before returning, bedecked with Elastoplast, to work at the study desk.

Since this conveniently adjoins the mews, through the keyhole of the connecting door, I was able to discreetly observe the owlets' reactions. Both were fully employed, pecking at their jesses constantly, and from time to time prancing around the floor in a frantic avian quick-step, attempting to shake off the bells, cavorting excitedly around the mews and sounding like a pair of demented Morris dancers having a fling around the maypole, in this instance the hawk perch. The evidently furious Phantom also gave a quite passable impression of the crocodile that occasionally accompanies such revelry, snapping her beak bad-temperedly in a distinctly reptilian fashion.

As the morning wore on, the tinkling of bells gradually subsided, and by noon both had apparently accepted the situation. At the mid-day feed, surprisingly, neither bore any malice for the rough handling, their hunched forms clanging noisily behind me like a pair of winged Quasimodos.

Now they were securely jessed, it was possible to allow the owlets outside again. In order to tether them to their individual perches on the lawn, I fixed a large swivel to the free ends of each pair of jesses to avoid tangling, passing them through the D-shaped end of the swivel, and looping each one back upon itself by means of a slit in the jess. The swivel in turn was held by a two-metre leash, the opposite end of which was secured to the perch by a falconer's knot. Largely unaltered over centuries of hawking, tied correctly, the knot is impossible for the bird to release, but can be secured and released by the falconer using only one hand; an important refinement when the other hand is employed in holding the bird.

The practice of actually tethering a bird may at first glance seem restrictive, even unkind, but the leash allows freedom of movement around the perch for a couple of metres in any direction, and in any case, the wild hawk or owl spends much of its free time simply sitting around when not actually engaged in hunting. Once fully accustomed to the limits of its leash, a bird will remain quite happily on its perch for hours, content to observe everything around it and seldom displaying any signs of unease.

Suitably attired, Spook and Phantom were able to spend the remainder of the warm afternoon perched in the welcome shade of the conifer belt, looking and sounding quite business-like in their new kit, their every movement betrayed by the pleasant musical tinkling of the bells. The initial arrested attempts at flight culminated in a series of rather inglorious nosedives, but they appeared to accept the fact that they were firmly tethered with the minimum of fuss, though at times worried offhandedly with their beaks at jess and bewit.

As the afternoon wore on, the air grew uncomfortably hot and humid. Although positioned carefully in the shade, the owlets were soon panting with the heat, enjoying a refreshing shower as I sprayed them gently with the garden hose.

The owlets revelled in the spray, arching wings and puffing up body feathers to allow the water to penetrate, and once the shower was over, flapping vigorously to remove the droplets before preening their plumage back into order. A regular soaking when the weather allows works wonders for developing plumage, greatly enhancing its weatherproof qualities and promoting a healthy lustre and sheen which soon withstands and repels even the heaviest of storms.

In fact I wash many taxidermy specimens during preservation, sometimes immersing them in a large bowl of cleaning crystals or even biological detergent. All too often in these polluted times, seabirds in particular carry varying amounts of crude oil and other dirt which is difficult to remove. A petrol-soaked pad of cotton wool usually copes with the worst of the oil, but even then plumage requires prolonged soaking to restore it to a suitable condition for mounting. A large bowl normally accommodates most specimens, but at times one has to resort to the bathtub for major cleaning operations.

On one such occasion, following a disastrous 'wreck' of seabirds along our coastline caused by severe storms far out to sea, I collected over forty dead seabirds along a short stretch of shoreline, the haul including fourteen guillemots, a dozen or so razorbills, several puffins, a gorgeous red-throated diver and a well-oiled juvenile shag, the latter a species seldom encountered, at least by myself living well inland. Almost without exception the birds were in a filthy condition, ingrained with mud, blood, sand and patches of stubborn crude. Reluctant to freeze them in such a state, I had managed to get quite a production line going, beginning with a quick once over with the petrol pad to clear the oil, a leisurely soak in biological detergent in the bath, a three-minute spell in the spin dryer and a final fluffing up with a hair dryer.

Occupying most of the afternoon, the job was almost completed as I kept a dizzy watch over the spin dryer, observing the antics of the diver, revolving with ever-increasing frequency as the machine got up speed. It was trifle disconcerting, I must admit, to watch a rare red-throated diver revolving at 1,300 revs per minute inside the drum; I dreaded it being torn limb from limb, but, barring accident, the spinner seems to work surprisingly well, saving enormous amounts of time in the final fluffing up by removing virtually all the visible surface water. There was only the shag to finish cleaning, already skinned out and taking a long soak in the bathtub, prior to drying out and mounting the following morning.

Suddenly a violent scream rent the stillness, emanating from the vicinity of the bathroom, where a female guest was apparently availing herself of the basic toilet facilities.

Had Whisper nicked the loo roll yet again? Surely not while someone was in residence? Had the guest been stupid enough to leave the door open?

Fearing some such catastrophe, Barbara went to see what all the fuss was about. It turned out to be caused by nothing more than a glimpse of the pre-skinned shag, whose proportions had assumed the elasticity of an emaciated heron, lying full-length in the bath with its long neck snake-like amongst the bubbles.

'Oh, that's nothing to worry about' she reassured our guest casually, as if such sightings were quite the run of the mill, everyday events. 'It's just Richard, giving his young shag a bath.'

Apparently, more orthodox households seldom utilise the bath for such enterprises. Our guest was equally surprised when, only minutes later, I conjured the partially dried shag from the tumble dryer, pristine as a new pin and ready for fluff-drying.

Neatly preened, the owlets also looked much sleeker, and with virtually all their body down now shed and replaced by feathers, it would not be long before I could at long last begin their education.

Before embarking upon the real training programme, now they had been jessed, I could at least begin to accustom them to being carried on the glove. Prior to this, any movement of a bird from point A to point B could only be achieved by picking them up bodily in my hands. Familiarising the owlets to standing and remaining on the glove, and getting them used to the motion of walking would take time and practice, the birds having to be taught to remain on the glove at all times, which they could only learn by experience; at first birds launch themselves – 'bate' – from the hand until arrested by the jesses, held firmly between thumb and forefinger, on the end of which they dangle upside down until replaced on the glove with the remaining free hand. After being replaced a few times, the birds usually catch on that it is far more comfortable to sit still while being carried, but this seldom happens until they have been taught to accept food on the glove; they then associate the glove with rewards.

Spook stood beside his perch on the lawn. Pulling on the glove, I crouched carefully beside him, placing my left hand behind his legs, while using the other to stroke the silken feathers of his breast, hoping to distract attention as I gently eased the glove against the back of his legs. Forced to move, he raised each foot in turn, and, without realising, replaced them on the glove. Offering a chick, gently I raised him in the air while standing up, but, realisation dawning, he suffered an immediate attack of vertigo, lost his balance and bated vigorously. A quick flick of the right hand under his breast restored him to the glove, but he bated again, clicking his beak in disapproval at being treated in such a manner. Following two repeat performances, he finally stood still, crouching as if to spring, but remaining on the fist long enough to accept a couple of titbits while I moved very slowly across the lawn.

For almost half an hour we practised, Spook making such good progress that I decided to take a short excursion to harvest some clumps of seeding grasses for my taxidermy work. Crossing the stubble field to the road, Spook bated as a car roared past, but when returned to the glove sat quite steadily, and by the time we reached the far side of the hill he was already becoming accustomed to the motion of walking, his grip and balance on the glove quite firm and steady. A couple of bouts of bating on the return journey and the round trip of roughly half a mile was far less trouble than anticipated.

Encouraged by the performance, I decided to compare Phantom's reactions to being carried, this time over a much shorter route to post a letter only a hundred metres along the road in the opposite direction.

Her reactions, even allowing her the benefit of the doubt, were considerably less favourable. She bated as I opened the garden gate. She bated as I walked down the drive. She bated when I sneezed. She bated as I dropped the letter, and again when I picked it up. She even bated as an aeroplane passed over in the far distance. In fact, to cut a very repetitive and arm-wrenching story short, she bated at absolutely everything in sight, from a song thrush flapping from the roadside holly, to a black cat crossing the lane 200 metres away. Dangling upside down in a fit of hysterics, she twittered with rage, her eyes burning and beak agape, as I restored her for the umpteenth time to an upright position. Her vertical hold was obviously on the blink! Having also reached the end of my tether, I was relieved to get her home. The hard work, it seemed, was only just beginning. At least I could console myself with the fact that she could surely only improve.

In fact she showed a vast improvement the very next morning as I carried her to the marshes to feed my waterfowl, crossing two corn stubbles to where the duck ponds lay beside a winding stretch of the river on the valley floor. Admittedly, there were few distractions to cause alarm. She bated only three times, remaining obediently on the glove even as I picked our way along the pond path through chest-high stinging nettles, already beginning to show signs of dying back. The little hints and signs of summer's passage into autumn were suddenly in evidence – in the trees, in the vegetation, in the autumnal scents and in the strange silence that seemed to somehow permeate the air, the bird-song now conspicuous by its absence after months of constant chorus, the stillness broken only by a staccato cackling of greylag geese and the harsh, throaty croaking of a heron, winging ghost-like above a slowly evaporating mist curling like smoke above the marshes. Gliding down to his secret fishing spot beside the river, the huge bird was quickly swallowed in the gloom.

Phantom displayed an intense interest in the waterfowl as they dibbled and dived for food, many of the drakes, after their late summer period of drab 'eclipse' plumage, displaying the first signs of moulting into bright winter attire. The delightful hooded mergansers were already flecked with traces of contrasting black and white, the young drake smew beginning to sprout his first adult feathers, and even the Barrow's goldeneye – a rare diving duck from Greenland – acquiring a hint of dark bottle green to his head, and white, porthole-like 'windows' along each side, the first steps towards full breeding dress. Not that I was under any illusions regarding his reproductive prowess, for I have been attempting to breed with him – or rather, from him – for years. He has developed the perversion of attempting to mate his female from the wrong way round, a habit which bodes less than hopeful towards fathering any ducklings. It goes without saying that it is an equally frustrating exercise for his mate; his more than willing spouse could consider introducing her partner to one particular mallard drake that visits the pond regularly. Well versed in the mechanics of gynaecology, the visitor certainly has no hang-ups of the sexual kind – rather the reverse – frequently attempting to mate with anything from a marbled teal to a most indignant drake red-crested pochard.

Spook's outing for the day was a trip to check the rabbit snares. He behaved himself admirably, despite frequent encounters with cars along the normally deserted road. We had no luck with the rabbits, but as one bolted to the copse from the adjoining pasture, he spotted it immediately, displaying a definite curiosity as it scuttled across our path and disappeared down a nearby burrow. Possibly, one day he would show something more than just a passing interest.

The bouquet had somehow been displaced from the rafters.

The following day happened to be the eve of our wedding anniversary. In the hope of earning an extra house point or two, I popped out with the truck and bought a bouquet of flowers and a suitably sentimental card to mark the occasion. On my return, intending to sneak in by the back door with the gift, I spotted Barbara coming out, just in time to avoid spoiling her surprise by nipping smartly into the mews, where I hastily wedged the bouquet over a convenient rafter, intending to retrieve it as soon as the coast was clear.

During frantic last-minute preparations for an impending all-night barbecue, I completely forgot all about it until the first of the guests began to arrive, and by then it was far too late.

The owlets had spent the afternoon outside. As the evening was warm and dry, I decided to leave them on the back lawn to test their reactions to the occasion, which, providing they were not unduly distressed, would do them a world of good, though I was prepared to return them to the mews immediately they showed any sign of agitation.

Standing still as statues on the floodlit back lawn, both owlets behaved in exemplary fashion, remaining so calm and unruffled that one guest, apparently quite sober on his arrival, at first dismissed them as extremely lifelike garden ornaments, refusing to believe they were the real thing until Spook, disgusted at being relegated to the ranks of plastic gnomes, concrete storks and one-legged herons, flexed his wings impressively to confirm the fact that he was indeed alive. The owlets spent the remainder of the night calmly studying the habits of the strange gathering of *homo sapiens* with apparent interest, taking little notice as the music inevitably got louder, the cavortings wilder and the staggering more pronounced, the majority of the guests severely under-estimating the potency of Barbara's punchbowl.

Much later, dragging myself up the stairs, I suddenly remembered my hearts and flowers bit. Executing an elegant three-point turn at the top, I staggered light-headedly to the mews, but was alarmed to discover the bouquet had somehow been displaced from the rafters and now lay mid-way between the owl perches. Spook and Phantom had already shredded the complimentary gift wrapping and, beaks poised, were just about to start on the flowers which, without timely intervention, would have been quickly reduced to little more than button-hole sized remnants. Luckily, Barbara was not in a condition to notice the additional complements of chick fluff, owl down, the odd wood shaving or two and anything of a less agreeable nature in her bouquet.

Half an hour later she had adopted a kneeling posture on the bathroom floor and appeared to be scrutinizing the rim of the water closet; in view of her pallor and exorbitant prostration, she was almost certainly not looking for limescale.

8

FLU, FEATHERS
AND FRACAS

A part from small, downy patches on the tops of their heads at which they scratched and worried absent-mindedly from time to time, at ten weeks both owlets were almost fully feathered. Following a thorough examination, I was satisfied that the most important part of their plumage – namely the primary wing shafts – had at long last reached their fullest extent. The birds were, in falconry parlance, 'fully summed' and 'hard penned'; the former indicating that the primary wing feathers had finally finished growing and the latter that the quills had drained of blood. At last, I could embark upon the training programme.

An easy enough decision at the outset, the original intention to keep one bird and dispose of the other was becoming increasingly difficult, as each bird became more familiar and developed its own individual character. Sooner or later I would have to decide between the two, but for the present, I could keep both, hoping that one bird would respond more favourably to training and thus make the decision easier.

There was by now a considerable difference in the plumage of each bird. Whereas Spook was predominantly white, heavily barred with black, by contrast Phantom was much darker, possibly more accurately described as black, heavily barred with white.

Shape and size also differed greatly: Spook streamlined and elegant, while Phantom, the heavyweight of the pair, appeared more cumbersome of movement and rotund of build. In birds of prey this often means that while the male is considerably faster in the air, in hunting terms, the female – by virtue of her greater size and weight – is able to tackle and overcome far larger and stronger quarry, though lacking something of the speed and agility to catch it in the first place. All things considered, there seemed little to choose between them with regard to any potential hunting abilities. Both were adequately equipped with the tools of their trade: razor-sharp, 25-millimetre talons for catching, holding and despatching prey, backed up with a strong, wickedly curved beak capable of reducing it easily to mouthful sized portions.

77

It was some time since I had weighed the owlets. As the entire training process depends to a great extent on body weight and the correct adjustment of feeding, it was now imperative to do so prior to making a start, using a chart on which to log and monitor the individual progress of each bird.

The prime objective in the initial stages of training a bird is to discover the weight at which it is at its most responsive. An over-fed bird will not lend itself to training until its body weight is lowered sufficient to make it hungry and keen to feed, hence the expression 'fed-up'. But starving a bird can be counter productive, making it compliant through weakness, which is not good for its health or training. A bird feeling below par is unlikely to respond favourably. Discovering the very fine line where the bird feels keen and willing to come to the glove for food – yet not over-hungry – is therefore the key to the whole training process at this early stage; the scales are invaluable in identifying a bird's ideal working weight. Once this 'flying weight' has been established, the first steps towards training it to fly to the glove for food can be embarked upon. Only by this method is the falconer able to exercise what amounts to a very tenuous control over a free-flying bird, which, once training has commenced, takes its every meal on the 'fist', thereby associating the glove with food and learning to return to it when called.

With lesser mortals such as dogs, one can bellow, threaten and cajole to instil obedience, but with a bird of prey such procedures would only have the opposite effect, the only method of training being the employment of kindness, reassurance, encouragement and reward, bestowed in equally liberal doses.

According to records of my previous hawking endeavours, as a general rule, an approximate cut in body weight of anything up to ten per cent was required to stimulate a favourable response. Although this might at first seem quite a drastic measure, it must be remembered that this is ten per cent of the weight of a growing bird that has been gorged to repletion – when it carries much excess fat, due to feeding ad lib to maintain rapid development; an adult bird needs far less food to sustain itself in peak condition. In common with all warm-blooded creatures – man included – once the bird has finished growing it is certainly far healthier on a sensibly reduced diet, sufficient only to maintain its energy and well-being.

After considerable difficulty and much frantic bating, I finally succeeded in weighing the owlets, who objected violently to being picked up bodily and placed on the perching bar of the scales, having yet to become accustomed to regular handling. It was something of a catch 22 situation. Before I could cut the intake of food sufficiently to encourage co-operation, I needed to know the exact weight of each bird. The necessary manhandling apparently did our relationship far more harm than good, judging by the conspiratorial looks I received after each had retired to its respective corner

Phantom tipped the balance at just under a kilo and a half.

of the mews immediately afterwards. Hopefully, this situation would be remedied shortly.

As I had discovered at the last weighing session, both owlets were much lighter than expected, though on this occasion, weighing took place prior to the early morning feed, when all traces of the last meal had passed through their systems during the night. Phantom now tipped the balance at just under 1.5 kilos (3.3lb.), her brother at 1300 grammes (2.9lb.) – surprisingly light – but, as I knew from taxidermical experience, the actual body of an owl is deceptively small when its feathers are removed, a great proportion of the apparent size attributable to comparatively huge wings, broad tail and a deep layer of down that provides an ample underlay for the fluffy body feathers.

Despite their weight, both birds carried an excess amount of fat, having been reared on a diet of day-old chicks, fresh rabbit meat and the occasional treat of a dead mouse or vole whenever my traps were successful. Mouse supplies had by now dwindled to an all-time low, the formerly prolific colony located beside the waterfowl food-store having succumbed to the taste of ripe cheddar and now depleted almost to the very edge of extinction.

Collecting the latest batch of frozen chicks, by way of a substitute I had purchased, of all things, a crate of frozen rats, though as such delicacies were an exorbitant purchase, they would be used judiciously. Thawed out and chopped up into unappetizing slices, the owlets adored them, delicately savouring each minute portion of the resulting disgusting mess and masticating every mouthful in evident appreciation of what was obviously the owl equivalent of nouvelle cuisine. Thereafter, I decided to provide chicks and rabbits as the staple *table d'hôte*, whilst conserving the expensive supplies of sliced rat for elevation to the more refined *à la carte* menu.

Food had now assumed an all important role. Only by rewards of food could I induce the owlets to regard my gloved fist as a desirable place. I would have to feed them on the glove at all times, thus teaching them to associate it with the pleasurable sensation of feeding, until the birds would come of their own volition to the glove for food.

Since the first associations of the glove are the unpleasant sensations of bating, a bird can easily become wary and glove-shy. Simply restraining it on the fist by force and carrying it about for hours on end – as was often done in less enlightened times – serves little constructive purpose whatsoever, rather the reverse, for although it certainly familiarises the bird with the glove, unless the bird enjoys the experience, it will soon come to regard any form of handling as unpleasant, thereafter treating the glove with the contempt it deserves. To make the initial contact enjoyable, the bird must be rewarded with food, but even here problems arise, as it will only feed if feeling confident and secure. All things considered, the best course of action was to only attempt to carry the owlets at feeding time within the confines of the mews, but even that was assuming I could actually entice them to feed whilst on the glove.

Until this point, both owlets had been surprisingly tame and confident creatures. Having recently graduated into fully fledged owls, their dispositions had altered; almost overnight they became wilful, obstinate, much wilder and unco-operative, and any attempts at handling inevitably produced a more spirited reaction.

Spook had obviously got out of the wrong side of bed on the first morning, bating frequently in a wild fit of tantrums as I gently attempted to pick him up. Although remaining on the glove for a short time, for almost half an hour he refused to even contemplate feeding, declining even a tiny morsel of the revered sliced rat, bating interminably as I moved slowly around the mews, talking to him in my most soothing tones in an attempt to convey complete calmness to allay his fears. This was an extraordinarily difficult thing to do. Bating energetically for what was possibly the fiftieth time, Spook eventually worked himself into such a state that he refused to even stand up on the glove, sagging weakly at the knees and toppling backwards as if in an advanced stage of dipsomania. My efforts to maintain indifference to such adverse behaviour can be likened to the hidden efforts of a swan navigating upstream against a powerful current: a picture of grace, tranquillity and calmness on the surface, but pedalling like hell under water.

The trouble was – as I knew from previous experience – a bird can often sense one's inner feelings, to which it will react accordingly to create a vicious circle that has a rather less than becalming effect upon all concerned. Somewhat deflated, and with nothing to gain apart from adding to his distress, I returned Spook gently to the perch; he had obstinately refused all offers of food.

With Phantom the reaction was little better. Though eventually condescending to take the sum total of half a chick while perched on the glove, she refused further offers, looking decidedly put out when returned to her perch fully half an hour later, still obviously hungry, from where she shot me a hostile glance before rudely turning her back and tearing sadistically at her bewits.

Hardly an auspicious start to training by any standards, but the one most vital lesson I had learned over the years regarding falconry was of the need for constant patience and perseverance which, in the end, usually paid dividends. A case in point was my first goshawk, Venom, an exceptionally wild hawk, who at first was undoubtedly the most exasperating creature I had ever set eyes on, but who in the end proved by far to be the most successful. During initial training she had bated constantly in explosive fits of temper, and on some occasions after replacing her on the glove for what seemed like the 500th time in a day, I was driven almost to the point of committing homicide. Soldiering grimly on, my patience finally paid off and we enjoyed an illustrious career of many exciting years together, her crowning glory the taking of no less than eight wild geese in fair flight, and an almost unaccountable number of lesser quarry. That stubborn old hawk had taught me much more than I could ever teach her, over the intervening years providing something of a yardstick against which to measure subsequent falconry endeavours and above all, instilling within me the basic virtue of the utmost patience at all times.

With the pressures of work beginning to threaten my carefully planned owl training schedule, patience was indeed a virtue in my taxidermy ventures, none more so than when my latest customer turned up, completely unannounced, triumphantly bearing the parchment-like remains of a huge dog stoat, apparently peeled with some difficulty from the melted tarmac of some hyperactive highway.

By coincidence, I had just completed the preservation, mounting and casing of his previous delivery, a well grown fox-cub, also a badly damaged road casualty. Justifiably proud of my endeavours, the cub had been painstakingly restored and tastefully cased, despite widespread damage, filthy condition, severe staining and a veritable jig-saw of broken limbs.

Having invested the best part of three days' toil to complete such difficult work, I was rather taken aback when, instead of the deserved compliment, the customer clearly expected 'something knocked off – for cash!', against the absolutely rock-bottom sum originally agreed for carrying out the job. The sole owner-occupier of some three thousand acres of productive farmland, this particular client habitually gives the impression of hovering on the breadline, and considered a sum that would just about cover the evening meal quite adequate recompense for my three days of hard labour. Relieving such characters of even paltry sums of cash can be comparable to removing a grumbling appendix. Unfortunately, existing business practices do not sanction the use of general anaesthetic when extracting payments.

Unbelievably, the stoat was in an even worse condition than the fox-cub, having collided, at the very least, with something along the lines of an articulated lorry. There seemed hardly an unbroken bone in its body: a disgusting mess of blood, brains, intestines, bones and bruises, with an ingrained daub of tar for good measure. The scent glands had also been comprehensively squashed. As if this were not enough, the skin had partially dried in the sun, the ears curled like dried leaves and nose shrivelled to the consistency of a baked currant. Severely flattened, it looked far more suitable for preserving in a flower press,

With my patience wearing thin and hardly relishing the idea of rebuilding and sculpting the mount into a presentable representation of its species, I also took into consideration the fact that, regarding any form of payment, this particular client had short arms and deep pockets. I gave, what was for me, a rather outlandish quote, expecting it to be turned down immediately. To my surprise, he agreed – almost too readily. It was one thing to agree a price, another indeed to actually get it.

Refreshing his memory regarding the original sorry state of his fox-cub that now gazed enchantingly at him from its fully landscaped case, he was eventually persuaded to part with what was, from his point of view, an extremely reasonable amount of cash. Removing a wad of newly minted notes the thickness of a telephone directory with some difficulty from an inside pocket, he carefully peeled off a few paltry bills of low denomination and grudgingly handed them over, leaving with a pained expression and his fox case after I saw them both safely installed in his brand new Range Rover. The hostile glance as he departed quite adequately conveyed that, providing he could somehow manage to struggle through and survive on the pittance I had left him with until the stoat had been completed, upon his return I could expect a rather more spirited session of patient bargaining.

Patient bargaining. That just about summed up my efforts with the owls. Attempting again to feed them on the fist in the evening, there was little significant improvement in the reaction of either bird. Although obviously keen and hungry, both refused to step on the glove as I dangled a chick enticingly, just out of reach of the perch where they stood teetering on the edge, ducking and weaving, head-bobbing and screeching, acutely interested though loath to commit themselves by actually jumping to the glove. Following an interminable wait, I picked them up. Refusing point blank to feed at first, by the time I had finished – well after midnight! – both had taken a couple of chicks, most of it while standing on the glove. At least this was a slight improvement.

The next four days followed a similar pattern with varying degrees of success. At least the owls were feeding somewhat reluctantly on the glove, though neither had made any serious attempt to step on voluntarily. Overcoming this first vital hurdle is possibly the most significant milestone in the training of any bird of prey. It seems odd that a bird that is capable of flying quarter of a mile with ease can find it so difficult to cover that first half-metre to the glove, but that single tiny gap represents a giant chasm in training which, once achieved, provides a firm footing to build on. In fairness, it is perhaps slightly easier for the more agile hawk, who can hop effortlessly to the glove, whereas a corpulent and comparatively cumbersome snowy owl requires rather more effort to move. But surely, this was not too much to ask?

Barbara saw precious little of me during those first few nights, even threatening to serve my meals in the mews and to install a sleeping bag cosily amongst the wood shavings. I had of necessity become somewhat nocturnal, the midnight training sessions by far the more productive, when all was quiet and there were fewer distractions to compete for the owls' attention.

By the fourth successive night, I began to make a little headway with Phantom. Untied from her perch, she followed me keenly around the mews, flapping, screeching, hissing like a blowlamp and tugging hopefully at my trousers, begging to be fed, flying repeatedly back and forth to her perch.

This gave me an idea. Holding my gloved fist on top of the perch as she pranced around the floor, I dangled a chick in front of her. Almost without thinking, she flapped from floor to perch, landing unwittingly on my arm. The reward of a whole chick was ripped to shreds immediately and devoured in a matter of seconds. When every last vestige of the meal had disappeared, I replaced her on the floor and tried again. Responding instantly, I fed her as much as she would take, my shirt sleeve liberally spattered with yolk by the time her hunger was appeased. Although probably something of a fluke, such a profuse reward seemed justified by her effort. No matter how accidental, we had – quite literally – made a small step in the right direction. Hopefully, at least some of the seed would fall on fertile ground.

Spook remained far less co-operative, progressing no further than a tentative nibble or two on the glove during the customary half-hour session, by the end of which, I was grateful, with throbbing head and aching limbs, to clamber wearily into bed.

The following morning I awoke in a daze, feeling distinctly groggy and wondering feverishly if I had been trampled by a small herd of bullocks during the night. There was 'something going about' in the guise of a 'flu bug', and I had obviously been on the receiving end of a major dose.

Forcing myself out of bed, I decided to complete the necessary chores and return to bed as soon as possible, but by the time the feeding round had been completed and the rabbit wires dutifully checked I was feeling weak, shivering uncontrollably and aching from head to toe. Thankfully, there were only the owlets to feed.

After untying Phantom from her perch, I was forced to turn my attention to Spook, whose piercing screeches seemed far more penetrating than usual. When I teased him with a chick, he seemed quite keen. Alas, before his response could be noted, a sudden bang on the back of the head sent me reeling. Phantom, launching from her perch, had caught me squarely across the back of the neck with the velocity of a well aimed house brick. Although somehow I managed to retain my balance, with Phantom reluctant to relinquish her vantage point on the back of my neck, I could do nothing except sink slowly and agonisingly towards the floor, as she executed the avian equivalent of a quick-step whilst exercising her talons. Having the back of one's neck treated as a pincushion by an aroused snowy owl was certainly not my idea of a joke, but when she added insult to injury by pecking enthusiastically at my ears, it was time to throw in the towel.

Collapsing to the floor, I lay flat on my face in the wood shavings, hoping she would step off voluntarily. Phantom stubbornly remained, wings mantled possessively, astride the back of my neck like a vulture claiming a gigantic kill. Clearly, she was quite keen for the morning lesson to begin!

Luckily, she eventually tired of the game. Leaving a colander-like set of widely distributed talon punctures on the back of my neck, she hopped nimbly to the floor, screamed in my left ear and tugged painfully at a strand of hair in the hope of encouraging a favourable response. Before the performance could be repeated, I managed to heave myself from the floor and remembered the trick with the perch. It worked. Twice she came, receiving a chick each time as a reward, the sense of achievement dulled only by the fact that Spook did absolutely nothing to emulate her efforts. Feeling overwhelmed with dizziness and fever, I finally conceded defeat.

By nightfall I had recovered just sufficiently to totter to the mews to give the owls their evening meal. Spook, continuing his role as the backward child, refused to come to hand, somehow contriving to steal a chick before pelting hotfoot to his favourite corner. Before I could even consider taking steps to retrieve it, he gulped the chick down whole, his eyes closing agreeably as it squeezed down his throat and emitting a complimentary belch as a token of his appreciation. Next I tried him on the floor, endeavouring to work a similar deception to the way I had tricked Phantom, placing my gloved fist flat on the floor between him and the second chick, dangled enticingly in front of him like a hypnotist's watch. Cautiously he sidled towards it, his entire attention fully focused. Barely noticing the glove, he clambered on. Lifting at the same time as I surrendered the chick, he began to feed immediately, completely ignoring the fact that he was standing on the glove.

Phantom was raring to go. Safely tied up, she was by now mad keen and straining at the limit of her leash to get to me, flapping straight to the perch when released, from where she stood waiting for food to be produced. Ensuring the nape of my neck was safely out of range, I placed the glove in front of her. Dangling the chick directly before her face until it had gained her undivided attention, I placed it ceremoniously on the glove.

For several seconds nothing happened. Carrying out the customary bobbing from side to side, her attention focused longingly on the chick. Suddenly, she crouched and sprung, landing with a heavy bounce on the glove and immediately seizing her prize.

Having gulped it down in two seconds flat, just to prove it was no fluke I replaced her on the perch to try again. An equally keen response. She had actually come to the glove of her own accord. It was only half a metre, but at least we had made a start. I could hardly have been more pleased had she flown a hundred metres. To describe my feelings as euphoric would have been a gross understatement. In fact, as a measure of my extreme joy, I even did the washing up without having to be asked before going to bed, Barbara having been forced to retire early with the initial symptoms of the dreaded 'flu virus.

Now that I had begun to handle the owlets on the glove without causing too much distress, they could be carried to the lawn each morning after their early feed, to spend the day in the fresh air.

On one such morning an inmate of the orchard, an adolescent marbled teal, discovered temporary freedom by squeezing under the entrance gate leading to the back lawn.

With Barbara safely at work for a few hours, I was indulging in a spell of well earned relaxation over a glass of wine and a cigarette, salving the very slightest twinge of conscience at such lack of industry by attempting some remote control photographs of the owlets. The attention of my subjects was momentarily distracted by something happening at the top of the garden. I noticed Spider the cat slinking purposefully towards the duck pen, evidently stalking something. Completely oblivious of the dangers of going absent without leave, the object of her attentions was waddling seductively down the path.

Displacing Spider with a well placed clod of earth, I rushed to the rescue, though missed the ungrateful duckling at the first full length dive. I pursued it hotly around the shrubbery, but it eluded me easily among a dense thicket of cotoneaster and a leafy *Acer palmatum*. But it was on a sticky wicket. Like a couple of well placed fielders, Spook crouched alert in the slips weaving from side to side, and Phantom, equally in tune with the situation, hovered menacingly around a rather silly mid-on.

Instead of declaring immediately, the teal sped towards the pair in blissful ignorance, its approach keenly anticipated.

What would have happened had it passed within a leash-length of either owl, I was never to discover, but luckily for its continued welfare, Spook, possibly in anticipation of an intercepting catch, flexed his wings conspicuously; the teal diverted sideways where an enthusiastic dive ended in the recapture of what was possibly an extremely lucky young marbled teal.

Occasionally I supply countryside magazines with photographs, and I spent several mornings observing the local greylag goose population with a view to a series of shots, particularly at the crack of dawn, when they flighted to feed on the surrounding stubbles, their wedge-shaped formations outlined starkly against a colourful and spectacular backcloth of the early morning skies. I got some saleable material using a long-range lens, but what I really envisaged was a few close-up shots as the geese whiffled down to feed against the dramatic dawn sky. Unfortunately, being highly suspicious, the geese invariably chose to alight in the very centre of the wide open field, not allowing a closer approach without taking off in alarm. I needed to conceal myself in a favourable position well before they arrived.

Next morning, armed with my trusty 35mm camera, a medium-range zoom lens and several rolls of film, the first glimmer of dawn found me cosily ensconced in the middle of a stubble field beneath a brown candlewick bedspread, the only suitable form of concealment I could rustle up that would allow sufficient mobility to manoeuvre in accordance with the varying approach routes of the geese.

Huddled within thirty metres of the normally deserted country lane, I was rather put out when a vehicle approached and, for some unknown reason, ground to a halt directly adjacent to where I lay. Of all the stupid places to park. This was the very last thing I wanted. With the car in full view of the geese and its occupant plainly visible, my efforts at concealment would prove a total waste of time.

Poking the lens through a small peephole in the centre of the bedspread allowed me to study the driver minutely, through the close-up end of the zoom. Quite understandably under the circumstances, he was staring directly at me, a look of incredulity etched on his ashen features, as he bravely witnessed the huge brown apparition apparently floating slowly across the stubble.

Hearing the voices of geese in the far distance, I decided to crawl across to briefly explain the situation, and politely request he move. In the event, this proved to be unnecessary.

Rearing up and shuffling slowly towards the vehicle, I approached beneath my candlewick canopy, but the vehicle suddenly whirred into life and accelerated swiftly down the lane, its white-faced occupant, glancing back nervously, thinking of several infinitely more desirable places to be in the half-light of dawn, as the ghostly brown shroud approached. At least he had been easily displaced.

The greylags arrived right on cue only minutes later, providing a splendid opportunity for a competent series of shots. Meanwhile, if there are any reported sightings of giant mobile molehills, or other unidentified terrestrial objects perambulating mysteriously around the early morning Norfolk countryside, I shall categorically deny all knowledge.

The white-faced occupant thought of several places he would rather be as the ghostly brown shroud approached.

9

BULBULS
IN THE BRAMLEYS

Now the heatwave had at last broken, there was suddenly a distinct autumnal feeling in the air; no more the harsh, baking sun and seemingly endless blue skies, instead a contrasting chill felt especially at dawn and dusk and throughout the steadily lengthening hours of darkness. A million stars twinkled like diamonds on the velvety blackness of night, promising frost, and a ghostly, grey mist from the marshes crept almost to the front door of the house, until pushed back reluctantly by a sun that grew daily more lethargic.

In the hazy, tree-dripping dawns, every bush and blade of grass was hung with the gossamer webs of countless spiders, their intricate lacework bejewelled with early morning dew, sparkling brightly as the first gentle rays of sunlight glinted in every silver bead and varnished the blood-red hips hanging heavily on the thorns, imparting a moist veneer to the bruise-coloured blackberries suspended on the brambles.

Despite the past rigours of the drought, mists and mellow fruitfulness abounded, enhancing the sights and scents so typical of early autumn, a pleasant contrast to the monotonous heat and desiccation of the preceding weeks.

Sunsets grew daily more spectacular, the western sky a riot of colour that defied description: constantly changing washes of rose-pink, ultramarine, apple green and cadmium yellow, blended together in such perfect unison as to be unreal. Coveys of grey partridges, closing ranks for the night that lay ahead, called rustily from the plough, and hordes of hungry duck from the lowland marshes flighted on whistling pinions to glean spilled grain on the bare corn stubble.

Strangely quiet, a time of rapid transition had begun, with many of the vast hordes of summer visitors already departed to warmer climes for the coming winter. The warblers from the now emptily rustling reedbeds, the whitethroat from his retreat amongst the nettlebeds, and the familiar cuckoo now nothing more than a memory of summer past. Swallows mustered daily in ever-increasing numbers preparing for the long journey home, the power lines a-twitter with their song, and closer to home the house martins struggled to rear the last of their third brood below the eaves, tripping urgently back and forth with dwindling supplies of food, their actions closely monitored by a pair of adolescent snowy owls spending quiet, relaxing days on the back lawn between periods of training.

A week had passed since training had begun in earnest, a week of little triumphs and failures, most of the former attained by Phantom, who was now jumping regularly to the glove for food while in the mews, and this very morning had completed her longest flight to date, coming instantly when called a full couple of metres. Now quite confident and relaxed while on the glove, she still had to be encouraged to do it all again outside, but as yet there seemed rather too many distractions to compete for her attention. Hopefully, it was just a matter of time.

Phantom had also, through sheer persistence, managed to work out just exactly how her bell bewits were attached, constantly worrying at them until I discovered both below her perch one morning. She looked so pleased with herself that I decided not to spoil her satisfaction by refitting them with stronger leather until it became absolutely necessary.

Spook on the other hand, was proving extremely difficult to communicate with, even after the removal of slightly more weight than Phantom. I had actually managed to persuade him to feed on my fist, but he was obviously far less settled than his sister, the slightest upset liable to send him off into a wild fit of bating, after which he would refuse point blank to co-operate further.

Thinking back, I could only attribute his feelings of insecurity to a time when, just after he had been jessed, I had carried him carefully out to the garden when a jet fighter roared low and unexpectedly overhead, sending him totally berserk. Terror-struck, he had bated violently; screaming, twittering with rage and panting desperately, eyes gaping and breast heaving with the effort, taking a long time to calm down even when placed on his familiar perch. Possibly, he now associated the glove with this terrifying memory.

I also had slight reservations about his eyesight. Obviously able to pick out distant moving objects with unerring accuracy, he often seemed unable to focus properly on anything close up, and even when feeding on the fist, fumbled and felt for his food with his beak, rather than seeing it, regularly pulling at the index finger of the glove instead of the offered meat. I had previously taken little notice when, after dropping a chick on the mews floor – where it blended quite well with the wood shavings – he often fumbled about for ages before rediscovering it, usually right under his beak. He certainly did not appear cross-eyed, but the problem was so annoying that I had begun to seriously consider a visit to the optician.

Possibly snowy owls were long-sighted, but if Spook failed to see the chick on the glove, there was no earthly reason why he should ever fly willingly to the fist. With regard to actual hunting, a visually impaired owl was about as much use as breasts on a fish.

Displaying obvious signs of keenness, at feeding time Spook leaned towards me from the perch, screeching hungrily, puffing himself up like a stag turkey and swaying from side to side, but never once actually committing himself to flight. As far as jumping to the fist was concerned, he displayed about as much co-operation as last week's limp lettuce. Getting anywhere at all with Spook was inevitably to be a long, patient, and at times extremely tiresome procedure and, with no guarantee of success, quite possibly a total waste of time.

As if to prove me wrong, a few days later he astounded me by actually attempting to jump to the glove. The elation, however, was short-lived. It looked as though he was trying to imitate a 'Fosberry flop'; he misjudged the target, by a vital 30 centimetres (12 in.) and bumped his chin on the glove on the way down to an inglorious crash-landing on the floor. Repeated attempts followed a similar pattern. Try as he might, he just never quite made it, seeming unable to attain the glove, placed only half a metre in front of his beak. The most frustrating thing of all was that although he seemed unable to gauge the distance from perch to glove, he judged his return from floor to perch precisely, flitting easily upwards, landing surefooted as a cat and turning immediately to face me, waiting for the glove to be produced again. Patiently I offered it at decreasing distances in front of him, and he tried again – and again! – at each attempt seeming to suddenly weaken at the knees and executing nothing more ambitious than a pathetic display of exaggerated bellyflops. It made no sense at all.

Quite remarkably, this was the very same bird that had, only a couple of weeks previously, winged skilfully around the garden and powered effortlessly away across the adjoining field; now, even though extremely keen to feed, he seemed incapable of flying half a metre, staggering off the edge of the perch as if totally under the influence. To be fair, I did concede that he was at least collapsing in the right direction.

Day after day it was the same, each twice-daily, half-hour session ending in abject frustration, the entire fiasco ritually enacted time and again with not the slightest hint of progress. Though he flitted competently from perch to perch around the mews, when offered the glove he immediately assumed the levitation and buoyancy of a lead balloon, ending each successive attempt by once again measuring his length on the floor.

Maintaining the slightest shred of composure under such pressures demands a degree of patience that only a seasoned falconer can know. Despite somehow giving the appearance of remaining cool, calm and collected whilst in the mews, at times I was forced to retreat quietly outside. Once safely out of earshot, suppressed emotions were released by kicking the nearest inanimate object and screaming at the top of my voice. Luckily, our neigh-

Phantom was coming confidently and well.

bours are reasonably distant, though Barbara suggested a punchbag outside the mews door was possibly a necessary addition to the conventional accoutrements of falconry where snowy owls were concerned.

On the other hand – at least at this stage of the proceedings – Phantom was progressing literally in leaps and bounds, having outflown the length of the leash and graduated to the 'creance', the falconry term for a long line, substituted for the leash, when training a bird to fly to the fist over increasing distances. Coming confidently and well for her food, she had now clocked up a flight of at least five metres to the glove in the back garden, where, despite momentary distraction, she was coming with the minimum of delay. She had developed the rather annoying and sometimes painful habit of landing on my arm instead of the glove, but this was slowly being overcome by altering the position of the glove just prior to the moment of touchdown.

Alas, after just a few days, Phantom too began to display signs of somewhat less than perfect eyesight, coming well and confidently until, within two metres of the glove, she lowered her landing gear prematurely and parachuted earthwards in an untidy heap, picking herself up, dusting herself off, and waddling in duck-like fashion the rest of the way.

As she pulled insistently at my shoelaces and screamed to be fed, at this juncture I really did plumb the depths of despair. There was just no earthy reason for such behaviour.

My only theory was that, for some unknown reason, snowy owls were indeed long-sighted; unable to focus clearly on anything close by. At long range their vision seemed perfect, evidenced by the fact that the slightest movement of bird or beast in the distance was spotted immediately and followed with definite interest.

Even this theory held little water, for when flying anywhere other than the glove, she did so with complete confidence and precision, landing exactly and easily on any desirable perch. Analysing the situation rationally, there seemed no logical explanation.

The wild snowy owl obviously needs good eyesight for its survival, locating prey at a distance which it pursues and pounces on when within striking distance; lemmings are agile creatures undoubtedly capable of elusive twists and turns when hard pressed, and presumably require deft and accurate footwork to bring about their capture. With defective close-up vision, surely the wild owl would find sufficient food difficult to catch? But survive they did, though just exactly how was fast becoming a mystery.

Attempting to train a bird against such odds was to be an uphill struggle, but what I lack in common sense, I more than make up for in stubbornness. Despite the apparent handicap, Phantom was increasing the distance of her flights every day, though I often stretched out to catch her in mid-air at the end of a flight. Prior to collapsing in my arms she looked most impressive in the air, her powers of flight and manoeuvrability improving dramatically with repeated practice.

To accustom Phantom to being carried around the fields, I now began taking her on my early morning walks to check the rabbit snares, offering food immediately she showed any signs of becoming unsettled at unfamiliar sights or sounds, to make the excursions pleasurable. An occasional early morning traveller got quite a surprise in the half-light of dawn along the normally deserted country road.

One such encounter was with the wild tawny owl that resides in an ivy-covered Bramley in the depths of the old orchard, bordering the rabbit burrows, whose regular dawn hootings were one morning answered by Phantom, who gave a hoarse though quite passable imitation of her smaller cousin. Thinking a rival had dared to encroach upon its territory, the tawny came to investigate, beating soundlessly along the hedge on silent pinions like a huge, ghostly moth until, spotting the giant on my glove, it conceded that discretion was indeed the better part of valour, beating a hasty retreat to its hide-out amongst the ivy.

If our luck was in, the trip produced a brace of rabbits and, as autumn drew on, a delicious picking of mushrooms to accompany them in the stewpot from rings of fungi sprouting overnight through the cattle-cropped pasture grass, particularly following spells of damp, humid weather. Our forays were accompanied by the constant mournful wailings of young lapwings practising flight above the marshes, and the shrill pipings of their wandering cousins, the golden plover. Above all, echoed the cries of the wild geese, their dawn music – to my ear – the most evocative sound of the awakening valley, as great battalions of Canadas, spearheads of Egyptians, and a vast army of greylags travelled in wide, strung-out vee formations to and from their feeding grounds, creating an unforgettable spectacle silhouetted starkly against the backcloth of the wide, watery dawn skies.

On one such morning, Phantom gave cause for concern. Discovering the main ingredient of a rabbit stew in one of my snares, I was crouching down with her perched upon the glove while removing it and resetting the snare one-handed. The falconer has to learn to do absolutely everything one-handed, even answering the call of nature, a decidedly intimidating business with a full-grown female snowy owl reposed on the other hand.

Strangely quiet and subdued throughout the journey, Phantom suddenly arched her wings upwards, stretched her neck and regurgitated the portion of chick I had rewarded her with for stepping on the glove. This was most unusual.

Arriving home, she was returned to her perch in the garden, where she sat quietly, feathers fluffed against the cold, wings hunched loosely and head drawn into her shoulders, showing little interest in anything around her, her eyes assuming an ominous, sunken look, so typical of a sick bird. She displayed little interest in food, and when I did finally manage to get her to accept a chick, within half an hour she brought it up again, completely undigested. Further attempts later in the day produced the same result, and on frequent visits to check her condition, instead of the usual enthusiastic greeting, she hardly showed interest at all, remaining virtually inanimate on the perch and paying scant attention to anything happening around her. Even Whisper, creeping up cautiously to risk an exploratory sniff at her feet, was totally ignored. Her nostrils were running, and occasionally she sneezed.

A snowy owl with a cold? It seemed highly unlikely, though something was definitely wrong. A flick through the ailments sections of various falconry books did little to alleviate concern, for such symptoms as regurgitation, sneezing and sunken eyes all foretold alarmingly sinister conditions. I was reluctant to call in the vet, as few were familiar with the ailments of wild birds, and any unaccustomed handling could only add stress and possibly worsen her condition. I finally decided to leave her overnight. If there was no marked improvement, as a last resort, I would consult the vet first thing in the morning.

Back in the mews, I gave Phantom a light feed of fresh meat from the rabbit taken at dawn, removing all the fur in the hope that the meal would prove more readily digestible. She took the meat quite eagerly, but to my dismay, an hour later it lay beneath the perch in a glutinous, steaming mess. When friends called during the evening for a chat, I must admit my mind wandered repeatedly from any attempts at conversation, my thoughts fully occupied with Phantom's problems and what, if anything, I could do to help her.

Following a restless and uneasy night, I was almost afraid to open the mews door next morning, fearing I might find her worse – or even dead! – but on peeping cautiously around the door, I was overjoyed when she launched from her perch towards me, screaming to be fed, gulping down a fair amount of rabbit meat before I put her out on the lawn in the sunshine where, from the workshop window, I was able to keep an eye on her throughout the day while half-heartedly mounting a tawny owl, my mind more occupied on whether or not she would keep down her food. Luckily she did. After polishing off three more small feeds of rabbit, by the evening she seemed quite her old self again: bright of eye, keen and watchful, and screeching enthusiastically whenever I appeared.

It was to be a rather stressful week. The following afternoon, while Phantom convalesced on her garden perch, as if in sympathy with her condition, Whisper, having been turfed out of the kitchen for scoffing half a tin of pilchards from the breakfast bar, rounded off the feast by consuming a large bowl of waste fat, admittedly left rather carelessly within her reach on the picnic table after Barbara had replaced the distinctly nauseous contents of the deep fat chip fryer. Although she seemed pleased with herself at the time and licked her lips with the self-satisfied smugness of a cat that has just stolen the cream, even Whisper would have finally admitted that it had been a mistake. Instead of spending the night indoors, she was banished to the goat shed.

This was not a punishment. That was self-inflicted, and would take effect in due course. Her isolation was more in the way of a safety measure, due to the highly laxative properties of well-used chip pan fat. Next morning, by the time the fat had gurgled its inevitable way through her system, when viewing the results of a volatile stomach disorder and an even more aggravated degree of flatulence than usual, the decision had clearly been taken wisely. Judging by the state of the goat shed and nearby garden, the blood-shot eyes, the queasy and exhausted expression, Whisper had spent an active night. She would certainly think twice about doing that again!

Next on the agenda was the bulbul. The red-vented bulbul – *Pycnonotus cafer*, to be precise – is a shrike-like bird, which inhabits the more thickly forested regions of Asia. One was, somewhat surprisingly, shortly to be abroad in the Norfolk countryside. My close friend, Munch, also an ardent birdkeeper, turned up at the house one evening looking extremely depressed. For the second time within the space of a few nights, his bird collection had suffered the attention of rats, which had broken into his garden aviaries to cause heavy depredations among the residents, the latest visit resulting in the disappearance of a newly-acquired pair of golden weavers and a tiny diamond dove.

In order to repair the aviaries he had to remove the birds. As one of our large aviaries held only a young pair of cockatiels and a moulting cock canary, it seemed sensible for the birds to spend a few days with us while Munch attended to the aviary floor, the motley remains of his flock including a sprightly pekin robin, the recently widowed diamond dove, a selection of finches and, his pride and joy, a pair of red-vented bulbuls.

Unfortunately, one of the latter, a scruffy individual without a tail and several outer primaries from its left wing, was something of an escapologist, managing to squirm its way to freedom on the very first day through a mouse-sized hole in a corner of our aviary. Once free, it called invitingly to its less enterprising partner; but, although this revealed its whereabouts, I could not manage to creep within comfortable swiping range with a long-handled landing net. After repeated abortive attempts, I decided to await the falling of darkness, when it would hopefully settle down to roost as near as possible to its imprisoned mate, making capture comparatively straightforward.

Much later that evening, stumbling about in the pitch darkness, I searched the outside of the aviary and surrounding bushes minutely. There was no sign of the creature, even following an extensive search of the orchard and – illicitly – the garden next door.

Fortunately, at first light the bird was discovered deep in a low, leafy shrub beside the aviary, and, its feathers waterlogged from an early shower, as Barbara flushed it from its hiding place towards me, it was easily secured with a deft swipe of the landing net. With the mouse hole now firmly blocked, the bulbul was returned to the aviary, having suffered little worse than the loss of a moderate proportion of its remaining plumage.

Either the bird hated confinement, or reckoned its temporary accommodation was not up to scratch, for three days later, only an hour or so before Munch was due to collect his birds, I was intrigued to hear the strange, unfamiliar warblings of an unknown specimen from the top of a Scots pine adjoining the snowy owl enclosure. Intrigued, that was, until a fleeting glimpse showed that the wretched bulbul was out again.

Grabbing the landing net and summoning Barbara from the kitchen, I instructed her to climb the pine in an attempt to displace the bird, while I waited far below with the net. As she ascended, so did the bulbul, hopping annoyingly just out of reach each time she neared, until Barbara was swaying rather precariously among the slender top branches of the pine. The stubborn bird, obviously considerably lighter in weight, had by now achieved the topmost sprig of needles.

With an acute shortage of wing feathers, the bulbul was understandably loath to leave the tree, but when Barbara, clinging to the trunk like a limpet, shook the topmost branches to encourage it out, the bird was left no choice.

At this moment Jennifer arrived on the scene, her requests as to the likelihood of an evening meal fading as she spotted Barbara swaying dizzily, high above her in the tree. There was barely time for her to exclaim an, 'Oh, my God, mother!' before she too was commandeered to join reluctantly in the chase.

With the odds becoming stacked heavily against it, the thing committed itself unsteadily to its wings, parachuting optimistically earthwards and propelling itself like a wind-blown paper bag across the orchard, to the accompaniment of shouts, screams and well chosen oaths as Jennifer and I followed hot on its heels.

Barbara caused an immediate and profuse fall of apples.

It gained sanctuary in the neighbour's apple tree – luckily quite a low one this time – and by the time Barbara had descended the pine, Jennifer and I had it quite effectively surrounded. Having once again unerringly drawn the short straw, Barbara scaled the trunk while we waited in perpetual readiness, trying to appear suitably business-like by taking a few deft practice swings with the net.

Applying herself enthusiastically to the task, but unable to climb any higher, Barbara shook the tree violently to its roots, the action causing an immediate and profuse fall of apples but leaving the bulbul still clinging resolutely to the topmost twig. Another extravagant rattle brought the remainder of the apples down, a veritable barrage of ripe Bramleys thudding earthwards to lay accusingly around us on the ground.

Luckily, I was just out of range, and equally fortuitously, the shaking even had a mildly debilitating effect on the bulbul, now hanging drunkenly upside-down by its claws from a slender twig and sufficiently disorientated to take to its wings again, seeking a safer refuge. This it discovered in the shape of a stunted, though until that moment equally generously endowed apple tree ten metres away, from where, along with at least thirty kilos of juicy Newton's Wonders, it was finally persuaded to vacate the tree. Had our long-suffering neighbours any shadow of doubt regarding the mysterious disappearance of their apples, suspicions would now surely be confirmed on their imminent return home by the now almost skeletal trees, but luckily a vicious swipe of the net caused an explosion of feathers and sent the bulbul off course from the next tree in line. With such a severe shortage of feathers, any aerobatics were out of the question. Beating energetically for the tall ash at the top of the garden, the bulbul was fighting a losing battle, unable to react to our spirited pursuit. A flick of the net sent it dive-bombing into the goose pen amongst another cloud of ill-affordable feathers, and by the time it had been picked up, pecking and swearing vehemently, the wretched creature looked decidedly bald. This time it was incarcerated in the front porch, first ensuring that the ground-level letter-box was firmly closed, to await Munch's arrival, while we rather furtively cleared up the orchard. For the next few days apple pie, apple strudel, apple crumble and apple turnover were to feature heavily on the menu with almost monotonous regularity. To misquote a well-used phrase – 'with neighbours like us, who indeed needs enemies.'

To cap it all and round off what had certainly been an eventful week, Spook somehow managed to rip one of his jesses to shreds, thus relieving him from the pressures of education.

A hasty phone call found the jess maker hawking grouse with the noble peregrine deep in the wilds of Scotland, therefore the jesses could not be replaced for at least a week.

Rummaging desperately through an old box of falconry oddments, the nearest I could come up with was a secondhand pair of extra large eagle owl jesses, rather generous of fit; following another session of bloodshed, Spook was left hopping in annoyance around the mews, with the jesses, at least two sizes too big for him, reminding me curiously of the first time I had been co-opted into changing Michael's nappy which five minutes later had drooped to hang at half mast around his knees. Still, like Michael's vestments, at least they would serve to temporarily restrict Spook's movements around the mews.

10

DISTRESSING
DISTRACTIONS

The advent of autumn heralds the reopening of the shooting seasons for all manner of game and wildfowl, and the beginning of a particularly hectic period for the taxidermist. Normal run-of-the-mill road casualties, aviary birds, and deaths by misadventure are supplemented by a steady influx of specimens from followers of *la chasse*, to be preserved and mounted as reminders of memorable occasions spent at woodside, moor, marsh and foreshore. A variety of duck, geese, partridges, grouse and pheasants begins arriving at my workshop, the latter of infinitely variable colouration due to interbreeding between the many introduced races and strains of wild bird.

Thus it came about that my old friend Dimpton-Smythe rang to inform me that he had 'bagged a really attractive pheasant' on his vast estate, which was 'pure white' and – barely worth mentioning – was as always, 'in a really good condition'.

My initial scepticism was borne out by a quick once-over showing the pheasant, when it arrived, to be rather less than perfect, its so-called white plumage so off-white as to present a challenge to even the most bumptious of biological detergent manufacturers.

Since its untimely demise it had evidently been picked up, put down, stood on, sat on, lost, rediscovered, passed around and examined intimately by each member of the shooting party, including the pickers-up, the head keeper, and most of the team of beaters. Fought over by the dogs, it had been retrieved, suspended on the game cart with baler twine, and finally sparked off Dimpton-Smythe's idea of dumping it on me at some later stage for preservation.

Aware of the futility of attempting to point out these minor blemishes, I saw my client off and consigned the battered corpse to the deep freeze, to await such time that I was in need of a particularly challenging task.

At the moment I had quite enough on my plate. With Phantom apparently back to her old self again, I resumed training. Since she had outflown the length of the back lawn on the creance, it was time to take her further afield to where, conveniently adjoining the garden, a few acres of short grass led downhill to the edge of West Lake, lying grey and mirror-like on the valley floor. Flying regularly to the fist, during a week of intensive training, she increased her distances daily, at first coming twenty paces, then thirty, then a full fifty, though on longer flights she struggled to make it over the last few metres, with the creance dragging drogue-like behind her in the grass. At this rate, it would not be long before I could remove the creance and fly her completely free. The key word was repetition, to instil indelibly the automatic reaction of returning to the fist when called.

If anything, she had now become almost too responsive, often allowing me to travel only a few paces after putting her down, though I sprinted away immediately she had reluctantly vacated the glove. Running hell-for-leather across the grass with Phantom in hot pursuit, I was treated to a unique lemming's-eye view of the huge hunter bearing down on me, a most formidable sight as she powered effortlessly across the field prior to thumping heavily on the glove. It was a most exhilarating experience.

If only the same were true of her delinquent brother, but Spook was Spook, and even the slightest modicum of progress was still painfully slow, though on the odd occasion he astounded me by actually flying a full three metres to the glove. Consistency was not one of his stronger points, and the next attempt would often produce nothing more ambitious than a vertical nosedive and an ambling trot ending at my feet, where he tugged insistently at my trouser leg and demanded to be given food.

For some strange reason I could not seem to develop even a fraction of the rapport that now existed between Phantom and myself, and Spook was rapidly turning into one of the most frustrating birds I had ever attempted to train. Only a masochistic streak within me demanded that I continue patiently until all trace of hope had completely evaporated.

There followed several days of equinoctial winds and rain, the latter admittedly much needed after the long summer drought, but effectively preventing me from making much progress in training. The harsh conditions brought with them the first harbingers of winter: great chuckling flocks of fieldfares from Scandinavia, beating resolutely into the stiff south-westerlies, thankful that journey's end was near. Flock followed flock as the dawn sky lightened in the east, their numbers often swelled by their small cousins, the redwings. Tired and hungry, the new arrivals dropped gratefully amongst the hedgerow thorns, to pillage the ripe hips and haws in raiding parties. The winds were quite severe, bringing down spectacular falls of multi-coloured leaves – together with what remained of the neighbour's apples – the gales at times too violent to even consider carrying the owls outside, much less attempting to fly them. During periods of relative calm the pair were deposited outside on their perches, but, with only brief respites between the showers, hardly had I carried them out, than yet another black cloud would appear on the horizon and I had to bring them in again. My efforts rivalled Barbara's optimistic but rather futile attempts to get the washing dry, a sudden shower having the effect of sending us both scuttling to the rescue.

Confined largely to the mews, to while away the time Spook made a concerted effort to remove the ill-fitting eagle owl jesses, his persistence paying off when I discovered him at complete liberty in the mews one morning, the pair of discarded leather straps lying in tatters beneath his perch. The made to measure pair had failed to materialise, so I made doubly sure to lock the door each time I visited the mews. I had also ordered an extra strong pair of bell 'bewits'. Besides jessing Spook, there was Phantom to 're-bell' – a rather prophetic play on words, as rebel she undoubtedly would – before I could even contemplate flying her free. Keeping the two owls in serviceable legwear was beginning to rival keeping Jennifer and Michael respectably shod.

The very next pheasant that arrived for preservation was, a notable feat in itself, in an even worse condition than Dimpton-Smythe's.

A battered farm pick-up truck appeared one day as Father and I stood chatting in the yard; it came with a request to preserve a gorgeous cock golden pheasant; closer examination of the bird revealed that something of vital importance was missing. An intimate body search confirmed that virtually everything else was present and in good order: both wings, both legs, a splendidly long and undamaged tail and elegant body plumage. However, the most vital part of the anatomy, namely the head, was conspicuously absent, the front portion of the unfortunate creature culminating curiously in a bloody stump of a neck, which would be difficult to hide in any finished mount.

The golden pheasant, which originated in China, has been kept and bred in captivity for many years for its colourful, though in my opinion rather garish, plumage. It has a talent for escape and in some areas escapees have discovered conditions conducive to their well-being, particularly in the Brecklands of East Anglia where numbers have multiplied alarmingly, much to the detriment of the arguably more indigenous *Phasianus colchicus* – the 'normal' wild pheasant – also initially of far-eastern extraction.

Despite a leaner build, the golden pheasant bullies and cajoles the larger bird unmercifully, particularly during the breeding season when its disposition appears to deteriorate quite alarmingly. It is disliked by gamekeepers for creating havoc amongst their breeding stocks, and during the shooting season I normally receive quite a number, mainly cocks, much prized as trophies for their gaudy attire.

'It's certainly a fine specimen, and in good plumage,' I acknowledged upon receipt, attempting to break the news gently that the client's bird was rather less than intact.

'But ...' I began.

'Ah! ... Yes! ... well, I ... er ... thought you'd notice ...' he replied with an

The client's bird was rather less than intact.

embarrassed chuckle, obviously well aware of the specimen's shortcomings, and now also of the fact that I was not one to have the wool pulled over my eyes.

'I ... um ... thought you could perhaps supply a head, and ... er ... fit it on'!

Regrettably not, at that particular moment, possessing a surfeit of surplus golden pheasant appendages, and a reliable source not springing immediately to mind, I felt I had to point out that the head of any mounted specimen is undoubtedly of the utmost importance, the main focal point, particularly with regard to cock golden pheasants, whose fierce, piercing yellow eye, shimmering ruff of orange and black, and golden yellow crest were normally regarded as indispensable in affording the mount a lifelike expression, capturing the very essence of its true character and temperament. Due to an acute shortfall of spare pheasant heads, this was something I had no means of achieving.

Father, who had been quietly taking all this in, rather tentatively suggested that it might be possible to mount the bird in a recumbent attitude, with the head tucked under its wing; although admittedly leaving a certain amount to the imagination, this might possibly suggest the specimen was intact. His brainwave was received with rather less than overwhelming enthusiasm. The potential client departed quietly without further comment.

In due course the long-awaited parcel of falconry equipment arrived, and we set about the harrowing task of kitting the owls out yet again, the operation becoming only marginally easier with practice. Phantom, reposing quietly in the back garden, was first, and, while Barbara held her, after a few minor adjustments to the bewits, she was soon sounding once more like one of Santa's reindeer. Her strength was now colossal, her grip on the glove vice-like in intensity, and even through the thick leather gauntlet, sufficiently disabling to put the hand within it completely out of action, leaving me one free hand only to attach the bells.

Besides the obvious discomfort to all concerned, I hated manhandling her, for fear of eroding her confidence in me. Fortunately, when the job was over she quickly settled down again, feeding quite happily on the fist and apparently taking no offence for such manipulations.

Spook, on the other hand, was rather less obliging. At complete liberty in the mews, by the time he was caught up and rendered relatively harmless, his lashing talons and spiteful beak had already reopened a few old wounds, but soon he too was kitted out again and we emerged, covered with dust, wood shavings and scratches, allowing him time to recover before putting him out in the garden again.

Besides my wounds, the struggle did very little for Barbara's new hairdo, but as I took great pains to inform her, it looked far better in the more relaxed, less conventional style. Miraculously, she had escaped yet again without so much as a scratch, while I was forced to retire to the bathroom immediately afterwards to apply liberal amounts of antiseptic to my wounds.

As if that were not enough, some time later in the day, while cleaning out the adults' aviary, the female, after sidling suspiciously towards me along a bough, suddenly took it upon herself to attack. Her unexpected and quite unprovoked swoop culminated in a hefty thump in the side of my chest, accompanied by a burning sensation along the right-hand side of the ribcage, which turned out on inspection to be a neat pattern of eight deep puncture marks extending from the right armpit to the bottom of the rib-cage.

With Phantom now fully furnished and flying well, I decided the time had come to really put her to the test by attempting the first free flight without the reassuring safety of the creance. The night before the trial run sleep was impossible. In the small hours before dawn, wide awake, I occupied myself by skinning out and preserving a magpie, carrying Phantom to her weathering block directly a fierce pink dawn crept across the eastern horizon, and the first skeins of greylags beat in noisy formation up the valley.

At such times, one fully appreciates the advantages of being self-employed, able to indulge impenitently in such sights and sounds and, working extremely flexible hours, the ability to plan the day according to its needs, largely unheeding of the clock on the wall.

Admittedly, there are disadvantages, mainly the recurrent shortage of hard cash, coupled with a monotonous stream of sinister brown envelopes cascading through the letter-box, but there are some things money can never buy. This freedom I would exchange for nothing.

And such was the case this morning. As the cock pheasant chortled down from its roost in the orchard fir, the last of the greylags cackled over, and the magpie mount gradually assumed shape and life, I was able to observe Phantom's every move from the workshop window. With each aspect of her behaviour so familiar, and an intimate knowledge of her little quirks and foibles, I felt able to judge her mood precisely.

Following the coldness of the night, she was obviously quite keen and in a good working mood, but as the sun rose higher to bathe the back lawn in its mellow rays, the wind increased accordingly, at first barely strong enough to waft an occasional leaf from the orchard apple trees, but by breakfast time, when the rest of the reluctant household finally began to stir, beginning to rattle the bare tops of the tall ash bordering the garden.

Wind is far from desirable when flying a bird free for the very first time. This fact I knew to my cost when, during my first exploratory fumblings in falconry many years ago, I had lost a trained kestrel. The delights of soaring on the wind had borne the little falcon out of sight, never to be seen again.

To ensure she was really keen, I delayed flying her until well over an hour beyond her normal mealtime, ignoring the urgent pleading glances towards the workshop window, and coaxing the magpie mount until every last feather had been placed in its rightful position. By the time I took her up, Phantom was as keen as mustard, bating towards me as I appeared from the kitchen door and straining at the end of her leash.

Placing her on the scales, she was extremely impatient, barely able to contain herself sufficiently for the balance to register her correct flying weight, jumping immediately to my hand and worrying at the fingers of the glove.

Removing the leash, I walked to the grass field.

With a firm grip of her jesses, I removed the swivel, twisting the slitted end of each jess to avoid the possibility of it snagging on anything, should she toy with the idea of clearing off. Noting the direction of the wind, with trembling hands I released her on the grass, and walked nervously away upwind. With a mixture of excitement and fear, I experienced the old familiar knotting of the stomach, a feeling endured so many times before, but one which remains the same, no matter how many times one goes through the process of flying a bird completely free for the very first time.

I was walking away from Phantom, the owl for which I had waited half a lifetime and with whom I had recently spent hour upon hour of patient coaxing, manning and training, until we had developed a tenuous bond between us, a mutual rapport that at this point, coupled with the fact that she was hungry, was the only link between us. Now entirely free, she was in theory capable of flying even to her ancestral home north of the arctic circle should she so desire. Striding away, I was utterly powerless to stop her; hence the weakness of the knees and nauseous churning in the pit of my stomach.

At ten paces, her bells tinkled briefly. Turning sharply to look, she was only toying offhandedly with her bewits. At twenty, risking a peep over my shoulder, she was watching a falling leaf dancing past on the breeze, but at a full thirty paces, I could stand the suspense no longer, turning to face her, raising the glove, and calling, eager to feel her safely back upon my hand.

To my annoyance, she was looking over her shoulder, her head swivelled a full 180° and full attention focused on the untimely arrival of the postman's van, crunching its way distractedly up the gravel drive. She stiffened visibly as his uniformed figure appeared, walked to the front door – more brown envelopes! – and back to his van, keeping me in suspense until the vehicle had revved noisily away and disappeared from sight over the nearby hill.

Suddenly remembering how hungry she was, she swivelled back to face me, and at my call, launched buoyantly into the air. Beating a direct path to the glove, though side-slipping on the crosswind, with no dragging creance to slow down or restrict her movements, she came faster than before, flying considerably higher than usual, and looking more impressive than ever. It was indeed a truly magical experience.

This huge bird, a capable flier and as free as the wind that sighed through the adjoining pine belt, now able to go where she pleased, who but a few short weeks ago had been even too scared to contemplate sitting on my fist, chose to come swooping confidently towards me, her massive wings fully outspread and beating powerfully to carry her to me, the journey lasting only seconds but seeming to happen in slow motion.

Gliding over the last few metres with landing flaps lowered, she almost overshot her mark with such unaccustomed speed of flight, landing with a hefty smack on the glove. Phantom had done it!

In two quick gulps the chick was gone. Overjoyed with our success, with far more confidence I put her down again, this time walking a full fifty paces before calling her off. She came instantly, gaining height against the stiff headwind instead of loping along with her wingtips almost brushing the grass, and although veering sharply sideways on a sudden gust, drawn unerringly to the glove as though guided by some huge, invisible magnet.

Brimming with confidence, the third and final flight brought me down to earth once more. Having put at least fifty metres between us, a helicopter – of all things! – suddenly appeared low over the copse, directly above us, its startling appearance and accompanying racket causing Phantom to cower anxiously in the grass. Arching her wings in readiness for flight, she scanned the nearby copse as a possible place of retreat. Above the clatter and whine of the engines she could hear nothing, my calls all in vain and drowned out totally by the din. She appeared to have forgotten me completely.

I need not have worried. As the whirring steel monster, encouraged on its way with a few unheard oaths, disappeared over the pine belt, she turned to face me again, bobbing her head enthusiastically as I raised the glove. She came like a dream.

The morning ration gone, Phantom spent the rest of the day in the garden, watched over proudly by her trainer until, hardly able to contain myself, I flew her again in the late afternoon, a faultless performance with the ultimate flight a fast return to the fist, covering well over a hundred paces. Another giant step in her training had been overcome.

Taking Phantom's success into account, it seemed quite amazing just how different my two birds could be, particularly brother and sister, who, reared identically, treated identically and trained identically, had remained as different as chalk from cheese.

Spook, slightly the elder, had at first been far the more forward of the two, but now Phantom was flying free, coming instantly and confidently and taking almost everything in her stride. Her brother still feared many things and was reluctant to come to hand, at times behaving in an extremely restless and agitated manner and seeming by comparison to have learned very little despite receiving the selfsame treatment. It was to remain a complete mystery.

That very same evening, Spook managed a metre!

Regrettably, the same pathetic level of skill did not apply to the male half of our resident pair of African grey parrots. 'Tickle' and 'Livvy' – short for Livingstone – now reside safely in a gated front porch, but at the time Livvy was temporarily installed in a corner of the dining room, where most of his spare time was occupied in reducing a generously proportioned tree-trunk to a haphazard pile of chippings on the floor beneath his perch, and amassing an extensive vocabulary of foul language.

Quickly noticing Barbara had inadvertently neglected to close the door to the kitchen garden, one morning, without saying a word, he suddenly took it into his head to go absent without leave. He had never been airborne for more than a couple of metres at best, so I was astonished to see him disappear competently through the open doorway.

Fighting the effects of a mild overdose of grape juice imbibed at a party the previous evening, I was unable to give chase with much conviction, staggering rather stupidly in his wake, but, in all fairness, reaching the stable door only moments after his exit. I peered hopefully around the garden. Surprisingly, he had vanished without a trace.

I summoned Barbara from the goat shed, and we carried out a thorough search of the entire gardens and shrubbery to no avail. With no clue to his whereabouts, and Barbara on the edge of tears, I could only suggest whistling his favourite tune in an attempt to prompt a reaction.

Following a few dispirited and decidedly off-key bars of the 'Mexican hat dance', our combined efforts were answered faintly from afar, a flood of relief sweeping over us as a winged grey shape with stubby crimson tail detached itself from a belt of Scots pines sixty metres away, launched

The broken bough sparked off a string of obscenities.

unsteadily towards us, and cleared the house roof by a full ten metres. Tired by such unaccustomed effort, Livvy alighted gratefully in the topmost twigs of an ash tree, directly behind the eagle owl aviaries at the top of the garden, from where, as we approached, interspersed with the odd swear word and peal of nervous laughter, the opening strains of the 1812 Overture emanated vibrantly.

Chatting nervously to hold his attention, Barbara instructed me to scale the ash to where, at least fifteen metres above us, Livvy progressed resolutely through his entire repertoire.

Though I was not particularly enamoured with the idea of recapturing an AWOL parrot fifteen metres above the earth, I was still in the doghouse for imbibing too profusely the previous evening and dared not protest. Beginning the ascent, I found the footholds few and far between, persisting, with sloth-like precision and at a similar pace, up the vertical trunk towards him. Although slow, my progress was reasonably uneventful until, oblivious to the infirmity of the next foothold, I almost returned prematurely to ground level. The resulting 'crack!' of the broken bough sparked off a string of obscenities from above, culminating with the polite inquiry as to whether or not I desired a nut.

'Oh, my poor boy! ... I'll never forgive myself if he gets hurt ... Be careful you don't frighten him!'

Not even a fleeting mention of my safety at all, risking life and limb as I swayed bravely on another dubious bough, hardly in need of reminding of the danger. At least the bloody parrot had wings!

Feeling heavily nauseous, I was encouraged ever upwards by a stern 'Hold tight!' an uncalled for 'Silly old bugger!' and an extremely sumptuous raspberry; 'Mummy's little rascal' was clinging tenaciously to a slender twig.

Conversing with the confounded bird as sweetly as possible, I finally persuaded him to climb on my shoulder. Whistling tunelessly in my left ear as we began the descent, he blew another cheeky raspberry at an understandably astonished eagle owl as it peered out of its nesting box on the way down. I began to seriously contemplate ordering an extra pair of jesses.

11

CHICKENS
AND COMPLICATIONS

'What have you done with my chicken?'

The question was direct, blunt, to the point and, it seemed to me, mildly laden with accusation. Being subjected to such interrogation out of the blue within minutes of crawling out of bed throws one off-balance. The distressed and obviously quite elderly lady at the other end of the line did little to enlighten me, rapidly becoming more tearful as the somewhat one-sided conversation progressed.

'It's Blackie!' she quailed, as if such a statement answered everything. 'She hadn't been well, you know.'

Mortified though I was to learn of Blackie's misfortune, it was some time before I recovered my senses sufficiently to ask her politely what the devil she was babbling on about. Eventually, almost speechless with emotion, the dear lady managed to fill me in with the details about her pet chicken – obviously 'Blackie' – who, having been unwell, had recently departed to 'a better place'.

This last statement was only partly true, for although Blackie's spiritual self had long since departed, at this very moment her physical remains were apparently winging their way to my door.

Some days previously, it transpired, Blackie the chicken had prematurely succumbed to some virulent internal disorder of the gastric variety. Having been allowed to lie in state for rather more than a respectable period, unbeknown to me, her owner had finally plucked up sufficient courage to forward her for preservation. Apparently Blackie was now quietly smouldering away in the possession of the Royal Mail, somewhere between the other side of the country and my Norfolk home. With unseasonably high temperatures nudging the lower eighties, and being unwisely encapsulated in a polythene bag wrapped up in a brown paper parcel, her condition could now only be regarded as extremely critical. Following such abuse, by the time she arrived, I rather feared the postman would be the one on the immediate danger list, some poor, unsuspecting innocent being unwittingly in charge of a package, which must at this late hour be in imminent peril of exploding.

Unfortunately, having dutifully expressed my sympathies, before being allowed to clarify the relevant details, the pips of the pay-phone bleeped. I had no way of calling her back, so could only hover in close proximity to the phone to await developments. Surely she would ring me back.

Lurking within earshot for the following half hour, I kept a weather eye out for the postman, but when his van skidded up the drive around mid-morning, there was only the usual complement of begging letters and bills, not the faintest suspicion of the missing chicken.

'Any parcels?' I inquired, with rather exaggerated nonchalance. After a thorough rummage around in the back of his van, I received a negative reply. 'Never mind, perhaps tomorrow ...?' Bidding him good morning, I returned within earshot of the phone, making a mental note to be well out of his way next morning.

Busy with the day's affairs, I had almost forgotten the incident when the phone rang again in the late afternoon.

'What have you done with my chicken?' it demanded even more vehemently; 'my Blackie must have got there by now!'

I assured the lady – one Mrs Brown – that I had, in all honesty 'done' absolutely nothing with her chicken, explaining that as we live somewhat off the beaten track, the speed of the mail is sometimes rather hit and miss though at the same time having to concede that poor old Blackie could probably have made the journey on foot by now had she been of her former hale and hearty disposition.

'Well, what are you going to do about it?' she demanded unfairly, to which I explained there really was nothing I could do, apart from diplomatically outlining the usual procedure which, had she contacted me immediately the bereavement had occurred, would have presented her chicken fresh, wholesome and hardly out of *rigor mortis* at my doorstep by overnight carrier, who guaranteed delivery anywhere from Land's End to John O'Groats by the following morning. I also hinted somewhat apologetically that if Blackie failed to put in an appearance very shortly, there would be little I could do towards preserving her for posterity.

For three more days I suffered a spate of phone calls, morning, noon and night, but still no brown paper parcel was forthcoming. I even began to suspect a leg-pull.

Even so, the incident had me worried to the degree that even the attempted training of a snowy owl rather paled into insignificance by comparison. At least I could understand birds – or certainly thought I could – until Spook suddenly underwent a complete change in disposition, his metamorphosis into something resembling a Jeckyll and Hyde character quite alarming, and apparently attributable to experiencing some form of extreme shock or fright. Trying to figure out and possibly resolve the situation, for the life of me, I could think of absolutely nothing that could have brought about such a violent transformation of his behaviour. One moment he would seem completely at ease on his garden perch, but then for some unknown reason would suddenly flatten his feathers, crouch ready to spring, and bate to the end of the leash in a fit of uncontrollable hysterics. At no time was anything apparent to provoke such obvious distress. Not only did he refuse point blank to even attempt to jump to the glove at mealtimes, but even declined to feed outside – an unheard-of situation. Becoming distinctly agoraphobic when on his perch, he spent most of the day peering furtively around as if expecting something to jump out on him at any moment. Virtually overnight, he had been reduced to little more than a nervous wreck, and thus he remained despite all attempts to console him over the following days, becoming so neurotic that it took all my time and patience to encourage him to even accept sufficient food while in the familiar safety of the mews, much less make any progress in training.

Everything we did had become a great trial to Spook, so much so, that very reluctantly, I decided he would be far happier left alone, abandoning any further attempts towards training. With the steadily increasing pressures of work, this would allow me to concentrate available time and effort on his far more amenable sister, who in contrast seemed to enjoy our close association and proved ever willing to jump to the glove at the outset of each training session.

Phantom continued to make good progress with each day that passed, flying free mid-morning and late afternoon when the weather allowed, the regular exercise gradually building up her speed, power and agility in the air; abilities that would be stretched to the limit if my childhood dreams of successfully hunting a snowy owl were over to be realised.

Progressing to the next logical stage of the venture, I carried Phantom to the low marshlands immediately adjacent to the duck ponds, hoping to test her reactions when confronted with her first moorhen, a potential candidate for quarry if I could ever train her to hunt.

We arrived just as dawn was breaking. We descended the hill to the low-lying marsh, where the first weak rays of the sun were soon obscured by a cold, cloying grey fog, lying like a stubborn, permeable shroud of smoke over the boggy ground. With visibility reduced to little more than ten metres, we disturbed little on our way save for a single snipe that 'scaap-ed' away unseen in the mists from a muddy pool, and a hare that loped off silently across the dew-laden sward.

Gaining the riverbank boundary, we settled down to await full daylight, resting unobtrusively against a rotting fence-post amongst a bed of shoulder-high rushes.

All around us, the marsh slowly came to life. Two dabchicks dived repeatedly in a swirling eddy at the far bank, a water vole munched meditatively at our feet, and beside us, leafy alders dripped wetly as moorhen fluttered from safe, overnight roosts among pendulous branches, their squabbles interrupted by the harsh, throaty chuckling of mallard whistling over unseen on rhythmic pinions, above the swirling murk.

Phantom flattened visibly as the ghostly grey shape of a heron glided low overhead, the huge bird spotting us only at the very last moment, which sent it into a fit of panic-stricken gyrations, twisting and turning with deceptive agility for so awkward a bird. A cock pheasant exploded from an ivy-clad alder above, showering us with icy drips of condensed fog, chortling across the marsh to the accompaniment of a bout of annoyed beak-clapping from Phantom, for giving her such a fright.

Presently, the resident herd of marsh cattle began to stir. Leaving the scant shelter of the wood edge, in single file they plodded rheumatically towards the higher ground. Their well worn trail brought them lumbering directly towards us, their inquisitive natures aroused by the gentle tinkling of bells as Phantom shifted uneasily on the glove. Mustering in a tight, unwelcome group about us, their breath warm and sickly smelling on the damp air, the bolder amongst them ventured closer and closer, until the nearest inquiring nose, sniffing rudely, almost touched the glove.

Such a close encounter proved too much for Phantom. Bating suddenly and without warning, she caused instant pandemonium among the herd, which, with flailing legs and flirting tails, bolted in all directions until quickly swallowed in the gloom, their thundering hooves and bellowing voices the only tell-tale sign of their movements.

Regaining the glove, Phantom soon settled down once more, looking distinctly pleased with herself for instigating such confusion. She was certainly not afraid of a few measly bullocks.

My heart missed a beat. A moorhen had silently appeared on the open grass beside us. Completely oblivious to our presence, the hapless bird strutted foolishly in our direction. What would Phantom do? Barely able to contain myself, I remained as still as a gatepost until the moorhen, still suspecting nothing, approached to within a few metres. Out of the corner of my eye, I could see Phantom scrutinising it minutely, and so I relaxed my grip on her jesses in case she should consider chasing it – though upon reflection there was no earthly reason why she should. My precautions proved over-ambitious; the owl completely lost interest as the creature trotted boldly past in stiff-legged gait, much less displayed any inclination to actually chase the thing. As her potential breakfast trotted off across the marsh, she worried absentmindedly at a displaced flank feather and replaced a wayward pinion. To be fair, such a negative response was hardly surprising. Clearly, my next course of action was to introduce her to the culinary qualities of freshly caught moorhen.

To the uninitiated, the very thought of actually having to teach a bird of prey to hunt would seem on a par with teaching one's grandmother to suck the proverbial egg; but even in the wild, the urge to hunt and kill for food is not entirely instinctive. Throughout the bird world, youngsters are taught by the example of their parents in the ways of securing their daily bread, as opposed to begging unashamedly from the nearest available human, as does the hand-reared bird. Fed almost exclusively on dead day-old chicks, mice, rabbits and rats conveniently butchered into mouthful-sized portions, the captive bird even fails to recognise quarry 'on the hoof' as it were, as a potential source of food. As yet, at least in Phantom's case, food was something that appeared unfailingly from my jacket pocket, as if by magic. The most sensible thing to do, it seemed, was to get her a fresh moorhen to enjoy.

With this in mind I ventured out at dawn next morning, bagging a moorhen easily as it scuttled low along the main marsh drain. In this area, the moorhen work together in a flock each day, often clearing as acre or so of corn each autumn, and are therefore regarded, rightly or wrongly, as a pest. If I could somehow teach Phantom to chase them, there were moorhen in abundance, and high time the local population was thinned sufficiently to prevent widespread damage to the growing crop.

Following an angry red dawn, the morning started rough, with near gale-force winds ripping multi-coloured leaves from the trees and pushing great banks of cotton wool cumulus across the skies in a wild game of follow-my-leader. Instead of taking Phantom to the nearby grass field as usual, we remained in the relative calm of the sheltered back garden. While allowing her to settle down outside, I rigged up the dead moorhen on a length of stout cord.

I removed her swivel and leash, and dragged the enticement past her on the ground, twitching it in what I hoped would appear a suitably lively, moorhen-like manner. Barely moving a muscle, she sat puffed up on the perch looking mystified while waiting for breakfast once more to be magically produced, eventually becoming so bored with my efforts that she tucked up one leg and fluffed out her feathers, portraying the very picture of abject boredom. Studying my actions with some concern, she clearly thought that I had finally taken complete leave of my senses.

Spurned but undaunted, I repeated the procedure, dragging the moorhen past her from all angles and at a variety of speeds, though none aroused her to a more than cursory interest. She refused to budge an inch. Obviously, such a contemptuous object barely warranted inspection.

Attempting to make the lure appear more appetising, I attached a day-old chick. Following the initial scathing glance of stony indifference as the thing twitched past yet again, she did an immediate double take, at last galvanised into action by the eventual appearance of her breakfast. Not a little put out by so many refusals, I made her work for it, twitching the lure away at the very last moment as she pounced, and running round the conifer bed dragging the moorhen, with Phantom in eager pursuit. After a couple of near misses, I let her have it. The chick was seized angrily from the lure and crammed down whole in a single, most unladylike gulp. Turning it over carefully to discover whether or not it held more goodies, she left the moorhen untouched, waddling up to my feet, chirping pathetically and pulling insistently at my bootlaces.

Returning her to the perch, I tried again. This time she was ready, prepared to comply with my little eccentricities if it meant getting a reward of food. Directly the moorhen sped by, she was after it, though this time there was no chick attached as an added incentive. She was learning fast.

Twice I ran around the conifer bed with Phantom close behind; I flicked the moorhen just out of reach each time she struck, an action that only increased her determination to capture it as it bounced along tantalisingly just in front of her. Finally she succeeded, as, with a concerted effort, she swooped hard as I turned the corner, snatching the bird in eager talons and locking on immovably to the improvised lure. Instead of simply letting her have it, this time I continued tugging on the cord, her previously dormant instincts forcing her to hang on with a limpet-like aggression.

Despite the indignity of being towed inelegantly across the grass on her backside, like a terrestrial water skier, Phantom refused to relinquish her grasp. The tussle ended a leash length from her perch.

By now irate, she began tearing savagely at the carcase, ripping out great beakfuls of black feathers and mantling fiercely over the prize as praise was lavished upon her. When I bent over her, Phantom clicked her beak in warning and shot me a distinctly hostile glare. The moorhen was her property, for she had captured it, and woe betide anyone or anything foolish enough to contemplate taking it away.

Strangely enough, after tearing out a moderate proportion of its feathers, Phantom seemed unsure about what to do next, in the end mantling over the carcase possessively, puffing up her breast feathers importantly, and squatting down upon it like an irate broodie hen incubating a nest of eggs, the now half-naked prey completely hidden from sight.

Tying her to the perch, I left Phantom to deliberate the next course of action while keeping watch from the workshop window.

For almost an hour she barely moved, but eventually resumed plucking the carcase again, her concentration interrupted from time to time to peer around suspiciously, in the unlikely event that anything should attempt to sneak up unnoticed and purloin her breakfast. Predictably enough, there were no takers. Spider the cat, prowling by the shrubbery, was certainly no fool, even though mildly interested in the smell of fresh meat. The two dogs afforded Phantom an even wider berth than usual, neither possessing sufficient courage to dispute ownership of the moorhen.

It took Phantom the best part of the morning to methodically remove every last feather until her prey was in an oven-ready condition. Having once actually tasted it, she attacked the carcase with renewed interest and by late afternoon almost everything had gone, even the head and wings, the total remains after she was gorged to repletion two spindly green legs, a tangled knot of sphagetti-like intestines and a profusion of black feathers scattered carelessly about the lawn. Swaying contentedly upon her perch and unable to even contemplate another morsel, Phantom dozed happily in a bloated stupor. I wondered what her next reaction to the sight of a moorhen would be, but it would clearly be some time before hunger motivated further interest.

It was not until the afternoon of the fourth day that the postman rapped ominously on the front door, holding an innocent-looking, but distinctly odorous brown paper parcel. Complete with second-class postage, it obviously contained the late chicken, whose state could only be guessed at considering the passage of time, lack of air circulation and soaring midday temperatures. Blackie, it appeared, had arrived at last.

The package was borne, with no little reverence and respect for its contents, to the back garden, and placed gently on the picnic table. With the extreme caution normally associated with the deactivation of an atom bomb, I began gingerly unwrapping the potentially lethal consignment.

Several yards of string, two layers of brown paper, a copy of the *Financial Times* and a Co-op carrier bag later, I had almost penetrated the interior: an ominous-looking black polythene bag bound equally and inextricably with string. The entire operation was something akin to 'pass the parcel', but with far more sinister connotations. The taxidermy profession strengthens one's stomach to accommodate most smells. Even so, I was hardly prepared for what met me as the final bag was breached, an indescribable stink assailing my nostrils and immediately appearing to encompass the entire back garden.

Blackie, confined in an airtight bag for the greater part of six days, had assumed the unwholesome proportions of a feathered basketball, her internal gases having reacted violently to the lack of air circulation, and now unrestrained, seeming to inflate steadily with each passing second. Even Barbara took an involuntary step backwards after appearing innocently around the corner to investigate the cause of such a smell.

'I gather Blackie has arrived,' she quipped, rather underlining the obvious, 'I hardly need to inquire regarding her state of health!'

Inspecting the deceased from a respectable distance, we were completely unanimous in our decision. There was certainly no need for a second opinion. The only thing that could now be done was to dispose of the body before – if, indeed, such a thing were possible – it decomposed to an even greater degree. There was no possibility of salvaging the skin. In fact, I would be extremely dubious of piercing such an object with a pin, let alone a scalpel, without first having agreed considerable remuneration by way of danger money.

A suitably remote upwind site at the very top of the garden was selected for the internment. Having excavated a deep hole, Blackie's mortal remains

An innocent-looking, but distinctly malodorous parcel.

were thoughtfully disposed of. Covering the body with a few spadefuls of soil, I firmed it down with my heel, the action causing the inflated corpse to deflate like a whoopee cushion and an indescribable stink to waft upwards through the soil.

Only minutes later the phone rang, forcing me to explain to a now furious Mrs Brown, apologetically but firmly, the events of the morning and the fact that there had been no option but finally to lay poor Blackie to rest.

Taking several minutes to recover her composure, Blackie's owner then requested that at the very least, I could attempt to discover just exactly what had befallen her poor pet chicken. During another spate of apologies, I tentatively suggested that the wretched bird had already suffered enough. I had respectably performed the last rites by giving her a decent burial, and it would hardly be fair to disturb her further. In all honesty, there was absolutely no way I was prepared to exhume the remains for post mortem.

Various grumblings, grunts and groans at the other end of the line communicated quite effectively just exactly what Mrs Brown thought of my prowess as a taxidermist. Totally disenchanted with my lack of effort, just prior to hanging up, in desperation she fired a parting shot.

'Well, at least you can return my packing materials,' she requested somewhat unreasonably, 'I'm sure that's not too much to ask.'

'But what use will they be to you now?'

'Never you mind, young man,' she retorted, as if to stop my prying, 'I'm always in need of wrapping paper and string.'

Possibly she harboured the desire to forward a similarly lethal package to some other unsuspecting idiot, but, obviously, mine was not to reason why. Agreeing to her strange request, I hoped the pips would curtail the call, but on this occasion she had obviously come well armed with coins.

'Yes ... yes, Mrs Brown ... Anything you say, Mrs Brown ... I shall put them in the post this very afternoon.'

True to my word, Mrs Brown's indispensable packing materials, still reeking stubbornly of rancid chicken, were dutifully packaged up and forwarded, using far more of my own wrapping material resources to ensure nothing unwholesome leaked out during the journey, and costing several times their worth in postage. At least I was now free of the entire unsavoury episode and could look forward to returning to something approaching normality.

That evening I received a sickly reminder of the day's events, when Barbara blatantly served up chicken casserole as the main course of the evening meal, but I prefer to think it was merely coincidence rather than a sadistically warped sense of humour.

Early the next morning, following Phantom's moorhen gorge, an enormous black casting of feathers and bones lay beneath her perch. She had regained her appetite, but the day was far too windy to contemplate another visit to the marsh. Following a couple of short flights across the sheltered back lawn, she was left on her perch, directly below the workshop window. I now sensed in her a different reaction to her surroundings; she watched every movement of the garden birds about their business, as if seeing them for the first time in a completely different guise – food! If this was indeed the case, I could hardly wait to test her reactions on the moorhen.

In fact I was forced to wait several days before I could even take her out, for day followed day of high winds and torrential rains, the powers that be drowning the landscape in a veritable deluge as if making amends for the long summer drought. Such conditions were totally unsuitable for flying a bird. Phantom spent most of the time in the mews apart from brief interludes between the worst of the storms, when I flew her in the garden for her daily rations.

Hoping to at least make some sort of progress in the training curriculum, I decided to begin getting Phantom accustomed to the pick-up truck. If we were ever to hunt together, the ability to travel around freely would open up many more places for us to seek out and explore together. Even this mundane human experience is one that has to be introduced gradually to an owl, by taking the process carefully, step by step, at first dispelling fear of the stationary vehicle, then slowly familiarising the bird with the sensations of movement and noise.

For the first couple of lessons, I did nothing more than feed her on the travelling block in the passenger seat of the stationary vehicle, opening and shutting the door at opportune moments when she was heavily engrossed in feeding, but, when she seemed particularly keen, I started up the engine, allowing it to tick over quietly while encouraging her to feed.

Following a few lusty bates she settled down, and although obviously anxious, was soon snatching the proffered portions of food from my fingers until she had taken her fill. The idea was to make any new experience enjoyable, rather along the lines of bribing a child with sweets to get it to take its medicine – in Phantom's case a fresh rabbit steak or finely cut slices of white rat. She accepted the truck reasonably well, so I kept her relatively hungry during the day, and the following evening decided to go the whole hog and take her out for a ride,

Checking Phantom's leash was securely lashed to the travelling block, I offered a particularly appetising slice of rat to whet her appetite, starting the engine and reversing gently down the drive. The crunching of tyres on gravel was not conducive to good behaviour, a wingtip slashing me painfully across the face during a violent bate, but once on the open road she seemed to calm down considerably.

Glowering angrily around as the landscape flashed by in the darkness, she accepted a further portion of sliced rat with barely a moment's hesitation. Negotiating corners caused some concern at first, but peering out of the wind-screen at the road ahead, she quickly learned to anticipate the sharper bends, and by the time we had travelled a couple of miles began leaning confidently into the corners with the finesse of a seasoned sidecar passenger, straightening up directly the hazard was safely navigated and peering around quizzically like an inquisitive nodding-dog.

When we encountered another vehicle on the narrow country lane, she clicked her beak in annoyance, until it dipped its lights, slowed virtually to walking pace and squeezed past, obviously quite put out by the inconvenience of sharing the highway with another vehicle.

Reaching the main road of the nearest village, Phantom was quite overwhelmed by the confusing array of lights. Having led a comparatively sheltered upbringing in our small country hamlet, she obviously found her introduction to the bright lights harrowing; everywhere there were new and confusing sights and sounds. Street lights, brightly lit shops, public house lights, garage forecourts and an unending procession of cars flashed by, but she rose to the occasion admirably, anihilating several large portions of the diminishing rodent. By the time we reached the end of the village, the unfortunate creature had been reduced to nothing more substantial than its hind legs and tail.

With my concentration centred totally on Phantom, by some strange quirk of fate our journey had taken us, rather conveniently, to the entrance driveway of the local hotel. Appropriately for such a wild and windy night, it was Hallowe'en. Managing to convince myself that it would be unfair to subject Phantom to too much at once on her first outing, I made my way to the bar. Unusually, the place was all but deserted, though as the evening wore on, a few late visitors turned up, and soon there was the makings of a respectable party. Between drinks, I emerged to check Phantom, who was definitely familiarising herself with the pick-up truck. I was greeted each time by such a macabre chorus of wailing, screeching, and the rattle of bells, that the cacophony must surely have heightened the hotel residents' – mainly in bed – awareness that All Hallows was once more upon us. Indeed, when I finally set out for home at midnight she was wailing like a stuck pig. With ominously black clouds racing across the moonlit sky, a chorus of banshee-like wailings, and a full moon peeping atmospherically through the tall, skeletal oaks lining the drive, the only thing left to the imagination was a seasonal glimpse of a witch crossing the sky on her broomstick.

The return trip was admittedly more erratic than the outrun, but Phantom behaved impeccably, appearing to enjoy the experience. I did, however, suspect a fleeting sigh of relief as we arrived safely back in the mews, where, by way of a nightcap, the final remnants of the rat quickly disappeared.

She began leaning into the corners with the finesse of a seasoned sidecar passenger.

My earlier contretemps with Blackie the chicken had faded to nothing more than an unpleasant memory when, days later, a familiar injured but highly irate voice quailed accusingly at the other end of the phone.

'You can't do anything right, can you?' My heart sank. Mrs Brown again. What on earth had I done? She lost no time in filling me in on my obvious shortcomings.

'First of all, you LOSE my chicken ...' she began.

'But ... but, I ... I ...'

'You then say you can't stuff her for me.'

It seemed of little use to further protest my innocence.

'Then you won't try to find out how she died ...'

'And now ... And now...'

Here comes the point, I thought. Horror of horrors. How could I have incurred her wrath even further?

'YOU COULDN'T EVEN BE BOTHERED TO SEND MY STRING BACK!'

12

AN OUTBREAK
OF OBSERVERS

The following weekend saw Phantom's steadiness really put to the test. Some teacher friends, who had recently formed a small bird-watching club amongst a group of interested pupils, were seeking the first venue for the inaugural meeting.

Being of a rather less than garrulous nature – one of the drawbacks of enjoying an almost hermit-like existence – I don't usually agree to such requests; this time I was caught during a rare moment of insobriety at an all-night party, and I had been persuaded to escort the young observers' club on a conducted tour of the nearby lakes, besides introducing them to our various livestock and explaining the basics of taxidermy work, whilst allowing an inspection of the rather less elusive wildlife in various stages of completion in my study. Weather permitting, the highlight of the morning would be a flying display by Phantom on the adjoining field; thereby adding a unique experience to the introductory gathering of the young observers.

Although the initial delegation was to comprise possibly half a dozen youngsters, a couple of evenings beforehand I was mortified to discover that membership had multiplied alarmingly, the latest head-count totalling well over a score of youngsters and a respectable contingent of attendant mums to accompany them in a supervisory role. The very thought of entertaining such an audience filled me with trepidation.

Confronted with more than six people at any given time, I am prone to an affliction of what can only be described as verbal constipation, but at this late hour I could only agree, the meeting arranged for mid-morning on the following Saturday. With any luck, perhaps it would pour with rain and only a skeleton membership would bother to turn up.

In the event, this was wishful thinking. Within minutes of the appointed hour on a dull and drizzly autumn morning, a small procession of vehicles turned into the drive. Emerging expectantly, the passengers of widely differing age and size began preparing themselves feverishly, pulling on anoraks and wellington boots to prove they had at least come suitably attired for the occasion. The young observers, who ranged from diminutive seven-year-olds to those in their mid-forties, were clearly out observing in full force.

Having mustered on the front drive, like a mass migration of leafcutter ants, the contingent trooped around to the rear, to the equal bewilderment of Spider the cat, who paused thoughtfully from licking her rear end, and Muttley the mongrel, who immediately wet himself and bolted.

Potentially the stars of the show, the adult snowies also underwent an immediate attack of stage fright, disappearing like rats up a drainpipe into the dark recesses of their wooden hut. At that particular moment, I would gladly have joined them.

By the time the observers jostled three-deep and expectant around their aviary, predictably, there was neither sight nor sound of anything even remotely owl-like from either occupant. Attempting to rectify an embarrassing situation, I unlocked the aviary, marched to the hut and peered hopefully through the pophole. Accustoming my eyes to the gloomy interior, I spied an owl firmly entrenched in each far corner, neither showing the slightest inclination of venturing out to be observed.

Somehow or other, I felt obliged to put on a show. An expectant hush came over the visitors as I squeezed carefully through the door, endeavouring to persuade the owls into a more prominent – or at least reasonably visible – position. Invading their most private sanctuary, I was greeted with nothing more encouraging than a glaring scowl and a blowlamp-like hiss from each corner.

Surprisingly, with an intimidating shriek and an aggressive arching of wings, the female took off, swiftly exiting the pophole and flopping heavily on the grass before the crowd, viewing her audience with an expression bordering upon contempt and executing nothing more spectacular than returning their stare, only rather more owlishly. Attempts to persuade the male to join her proved entirely fruitless. Having backed himself irretrievably into a corner, short of physically booting him out of the shed, there was little to be done. Conversation regarding a stubbornly immobile snowy owl was soon exhausted, when she rudely turned her back to signal that the audience, singularly unimpressive though it had been, was over.

I searched around for an item of interest. The rare Hawaiian geese, normally quite extrovert characters, had retired unobligingly to the extreme far corner of their enclosure, the only sign of their existence an occasional muffled outburst from the gander. Luckily, the garrulous flock of red-breasted geese provided something of a diversion, but all too soon it became apparent that the young observers' interest had seriously begun to waver.

Desperately hoping for better things, the next item on the agenda was a nature ramble encompassing the nearby lakes, though it was hardly an opportune time of year for discovering much of interest. During spring and summer – and even winter – the lake and its surroundings attract a host of readily observable wildlife, the entire place literally alive with countless marsh birds, wildfowl and waders, including an active breeding colony of terns, many species of waterfowl and a couple of pairs of oystercatchers which regularly nest in the vicinity. On suitable days virtually anything is liable to turn up. Even the occasional migrating osprey on its spring and early autumn passage can grace the lakes with its presence for a day or two.

Much as expected, this particular morning, with a stubborn blue-grey mist hanging along the valley, there was far less cause for enthusiasm. Leading the strung-out crocodile of visitors down the lane to the lake, the entire place gave the impression of being totally uninhabited.

An intimate and exhaustive search with binoculars revealed nothing more impressive than a handful of miscellaneous, heavily moulting gulls floating lazily above the causeway, and a dozen cormorants huddled disconsolately on a sandbank fully a quarter of a mile away, their hunched grey-black forms barely discernible at such a distance in the mist, remaining as lifeless as gateposts as they digested the results of an early morning fishing trip.

Nine times out of ten, I could guarantee the glimpse of a kingfisher at the nearby carp pool. This morning was clearly the exception, the only vestige of life a brief swirl beside the reedmace stems, where nothing more exciting than a juvenile coot had recently retreated to cover. Even the carp that roll and cleave the surface with huge dorsals had temporarily absented themselves, on such a day lying semi-torpid and immobile at the bottom of murky holes.

By now, it was becoming painfully obvious that the induction of the young observers was turning into a disaster. Somewhat dispiritedly, we trooped back to the house in disjointed huddles to attempt a last-ditch remedy of the situation by flying Phantom. If things carried on the way they were going, she would probably clear off the very moment I released her from the glove.

Mercifully, Phantom's flying proved to be the climax of the morning. Already an hour overdue for the morning feed, she was keen to fly, digging her talons convulsively into the glove while being carried, our journey to the field closely monitored by a mass of youthful heads, framed in honeycomb-like layers, at every available window of the house.

Ignoring the exposure, Phantom behaved impeccably, coming to the fist immediately each time I offered food, displaying an impressive turn of wings to an attentive audience, who by now had livened up and were gesticulating animatedly as they jostled amongst themselves to obtain a better view.

Following half a dozen faultless flights we returned to the garden, where she was tethered to her weathering block to allow more detailed observation from the kitchen window. Having broken the ice at last, the questions began to flow thick and fast, the visit rounded off with a tour of the study. With a collection of well over a hundred stuffed specimens, here at least the students could obtain really close-up views of a wide diversity of wildlife,

The young observers' interest had seriously begun to waver.

combined with an explanation of the process of taxidermy illustrated by a selection of mounts in various stages of completion. The greatest interest was shown in the less palatable aspects of the craft, many displaying a rather macabre fascination in the array of surgical scalpels, syringes, artery forceps, glass eyes, artificial tongues and ear liners laid out for their perusal. A particularly intriguing instrument was my favourite brain spoon, a self-explanatory and indispensable little tool for the removal of grey matter from a specimen's skull cavity. At last conversation was flowing easily despite my earlier misgivings, and all too soon it was time for their departure.

Presenting me with a profuse vote of thanks, a round of applause and a very acceptable bottle of wine, with obvious reluctance the crowd dispersed. Thanks almost entirely to Phantom, the founder members of the young observers' club had been quite favourably impressed.

The weather had certainly taken a turn for the worse as winter loomed ahead, but I continued to fly Phantom at least twice daily, building up her speed, muscle and powers of manoeuvrability in the air. This constant practice, besides being hugely enjoyable, was vital if I were ever to achieve my boyhood objective and get Phantom actually to capture something. Strangely, this seemed rather less important than before, the thrill of simply flying such a huge and impressive bird almost reward in itself for the many hours of training.

Taking into account the fact that Phantom was built rather more for comfort than for speed, the pursuit and capture of some form of wild quarry would certainly not be achieved easily. Pheasants were too fast, pigeons out of the question, rabbits too elusive and lemmings, her staple, comparatively easy to catch diet in the wild, non-existent. For such a cumbersome novice, moorhens seemed the only logical quarry, being relatively slow in flight, over-abundant on the nearby marshes, and in need of drastic culling to reduce the amount of damage currently being caused to the growing crops. On the first couple of occasions we ventured to the marsh, the weather thwarted our efforts: a succession of misty mornings turning to drizzle, the drizzle to light rain, and the light rain to steady downpour, dampening both our enthusiasm and Phantom's plumage, making competent flight extremely difficult, and actual hunting virtually impossible.

Finally the wet weather relented, the leaden skies turning bright and clear late one afternoon to bring the chilling crispness of sharp overnight frost. Next morning, the sun rose like a glowing, frosted orange to the east, bejewelling the fields and hedgerows with frozen dewdrops. With hardly a breath of wind as I fed the waterfowl at dawn, conditions at last seemed ideal for a trial run. After allowing the strengthening sun a couple of hours to clear the overnight dampness from dripping vegetation, I returned mid-morning to the marsh with Phantom on my fist.

Approaching the marsh boundary, a moorhen sneaked unobtrusively into a rush-bed bordering the main drainage ditch – a good area of open ground over which to attempt a flight. Keen and hungry after a foodless night, Phantom had obviously also seen it, bobbing her head for a better view and shifting impatiently on the glove, leg-bells tinkling briefly and wings parting slightly as if in anticipation of flight. Reaching the edge of the rushes at the top of the ditch, I checked my grip on the jesses and raised her aloft, rustling the undergrowth with my foot in the hope of flushing the moorhen.

There was not long to wait. Bursting from the far side of the rushes, the moorhen attempted escape. Phantom, keen to secure a more physical contact, bated at it immediately. This proved a totally useless exercise, for in the heat of the moment she forgot to release her grip on the glove, the strength of the bate dragging me down the drain bank as she hung suspended, upside down, flapping madly, and shrieking at the top her voice.

Desperately I groped for something to arrest our descent, my free hand clutching at a clump of sedges halfway down the bank. I should have known better!

The searing hot pain as the sedges cut almost to the bone was only marginally less shocking than the two bootfuls of icy water as I slid into the ditch, but luckily, Phantom let go at last, landing beak-first in an undignified heap of malevolence, glaring at me madly as if the whole episode was entirely my fault. Without mentioning any names, she was clearly aware that at least one of us had forgotten to let go!

Following a reasonable interval to clamber out of the ditch, attempt to stem the flow of blood and recover my composure, I was allowed to take Phantom back on the glove. Frustrated though undaunted, we continued the hunt.

Twenty metres further along the ditch, another moorhen burst from the rushes. This time, as she bated, I twisted the glove to disengage Phantom's talons, almost throwing her in the wake of the moorhen as it headed swiftly towards the duckponds. Phantom followed eagerly.

Reaching the wire netting perimeter fence ten metres ahead, instead of relying on its wings, the moorhen choose to drop into the next available cover, an impenetrable patch of brambles. Only seconds later, Phantom arrived, over-shooting the mark by several metres and seemingly oblivious of the fence, directly in her path of flight.

I cringed in anticipation as she hit the wire, trampolining backwards and landing somewhat predictably in the ditch. As the ripples gradually subsided, on reaching the spot I was relieved to find her, although thoroughly drenched, peering around with nothing worse than a dazed and puzzled expression. Nonetheless, it signalled the end of any hunting for the day, the pair of us soaked to the skin and frozen stiff from the waist downwards.

My next encounter with a snowy owl was even more uncomfortable. Following another abortive search for moorhen on the marshes, I had just finished giving Phantom her evening rations when the phone rang. The caller, who in his spare time supplies dead day-old chicks, captive-bred rats and mice, and other culinary delicacies to the raptor-keeping fraternity, related the news that amongst his collection of owls, an adult female snowy had just given up the ghost. Reluctant to bury such a beautiful bird, he offered the mortal remains for taxidermy work, though warned of their rather less than perfect condition. Despite this, I readily accepted, for it is surprising what can be achieved by careful cleaning, repairing and general tidying-up of plumage. Needing the carcase in at least a fresh and wholesome condition, I agreed to collect it within the hour, though a round trip of over seventy miles was involved, made worse by a thickening fog that had descended with the coming of darkness.

When Michael and I finally arrived, we were invited into the welcoming warmth of the kitchen, where we discovered the deceased reverently laid out in the centre of the dining table, allowing the family to pay their last respects. Besides being quite obviously dead, the poor old girl was in extremely bad shape, the body soiled and emaciated, the plumage tattered and frayed. As a result of a long illness she had failed to complete the normal annual moult, the primary wing and tail shafts irreparably damaged by a year's wear and tear, greatly aggravated by the fact that she had spent most of this time hopping pathetically about the aviary floor, the entire lower half of the body becoming thickly encrusted with mud during the recent rains. It remained to be seen whether she could be restored to a lifelike condition.

After some time closely examining the body, I became aware of an itching sensation about my lower arms: a sensation that was spreading slowly and mysteriously beyond the elbows. Close inspection revealed a veritable army of minute lice, which, like rats deserting a sinking ship as the body cooled, swarmed wholesale up the inside of my sleeves. Striving to gain the warmth and security of my armpits, even as I watched, huge numbers appeared en masse from the body to swell the ranks.

Most wild birds are unwilling hosts to a certain amount of body parasites of some form or another – both internally and externally – but this poor old owl was literally crawling with them. Word had quickly spread that warmer quarters were close at hand, and literally thousands were beginning to transfer their attention to Michael, busily engrossed in giving the prostrate owl a quick once-over in case a second opinion was required.

Removing Michael to a respectable distance, I pointed out the invasion to my host. His wife, clearly reluctant to share the dining table with uninvited guests, quickly dispatched him for a plastic dustbin liner in which to encompass the owl, and also what remained of its dependents. This achieved about as much as shutting the proverbial stable door. Scratching uncontrollably, we bid a hasty good night, the immediate intention being to return home as quickly as possible, deposit the owl in the deep freeze, and douse ourselves in a steaming hot bath.

With attendant retinues of lice about our persons, the journey home seemed interminable, our bodies tingling with something akin to prickly heat. Scratching feverishly, I could feel them moving about in my hair, in my beard, in my eyes and under my arms, and obviously with no inhibitions whatsoever, beginning to invade even the more isolated and intimate regions of my anatomy. At long last we turned gratefully into the drive, pausing only to place the owl in the deep freeze before rushing to the bathroom and turning the taps full on.

After thoroughly drenching Michael and searching ape-like through his hair, I sank gratefully into the water, the immersion causing an immediate scum of insects on the surface, forced to vacate the refuge of my nether regions. Washing my hair added greatly to their numbers, and well before I was satisfied that every single one had been removed, the contents of the bath were truly horrific. Even so, I spent a far from restful night, the very thought of playing host to such uncountable legions causing me to itch and scratch well into the early hours.

Following a stinging frost, the next bright dawn prompted me to take Phantom on my early morning trip to feed the waterfowl. Calm, clear and biting cold, there were moorhen everywhere across the marsh, their black forms clearly visible against the whiteness of frost. Together with a bunch of mallard and a wary heron, most fled for the nearby river as we approached, but a couple disappeared conveniently into an isolated patch of withering sedges bordering a gently bubbling spring, an ideal spot to chance our luck.

Approaching by a roundabout route, I placed myself strategically between the sedge bed and the river and began working out the cover towards open ground, where there was less chance of anything eluding her amongst thick cover, except in fair flight. Halfway through the sedges, my foot sank into a hole of muddy water, releasing a sickly stream of methane with bubbles of marsh gas.

The moorhen chose this very moment to fly out. Overbalancing almost flat on my face, desperately I threw Phantom in its wake.

Phantom flew for all she was worth.

I saw little of the ensuing flight, as I extricated myself from the clinging marsh; glancing in the direction of the sound of receding bells, I was just in time to see the moorhen drop like a stone for a bed of brambles sixty metres distant. Phantom's stoop came just too late, her talons raking the air a fraction behind the moorhen – so near, yet so far. Gliding to alight on a convenient fence post overlooking the brambles, she peered keenly amongst the vegetation for a glimpse of her hidden quarry, her attentions divided between it and a few stray heifers that had rushed over to investigate.

I forded a waist-level ditch, and struggled painfully through a blackthorn clump to come up almost beside her, trying, breathlessly, to decide the best course of action.

Leaving Phantom on her vantage point, I thrashed among the brambles in her direction, hoping to flush the moorhen directly in her path. A commotion of wings beside me, and the bird reappeared. Struggling to break free of the tangled thorns, its exit was confused. Phantom swooped immediately, diving past me in a determined manner, only metres behind her prey. Somewhat disorientated, the moorhen seemed undecided which way to go. Setting off across open ground, at the last moment, aware of the pursuit, it turned for the river. This moment of indecision proved its downfall.

Phantom, having already gathered speed, flew for all she was worth, her frenzied flapping bringing her almost within striking range. A short glide and, swooping determinedly, the huge feet went forward. A quick snatch – and she had it, the pair crashing heavily to earth, almost lost from sight amongst browning sedges. She had done it.

Wildly excited, I waded back across the stream, another icy soaking totally ignored in the heat of the moment. Reaching the spot, I crept in quietly towards her, praising her profusely for the flight and barely able to believe my eyes. She stood before me, wings mantled possessively over the moorhen; as far as I knew, this was the first time a snowy owl had been trained, flown and hunted in a successful partnership of bird and man.

The heifers grouped suspiciously around us, their breath warm and sickly on the cold morning air. Phantom ignored them totally, her entire attention focused only upon her capture. Almost beside myself with elation, I flopped down heavily beside her in the soaking rushes, and with trembling hands, lit a cigarette.

Weak with emotion, soaking wet, scratched and bleeding, stung with nettles, feet and hands numbed with cold and clothes bespattered with stinking marsh mud – I had seldom been happier.

Nothing – nobody – could ever deny us this moment of glory!

My snowy owl season has now passed, as has that first winter, the inclement times over as spring unfolds with steadily lengthening hours of daylight, each new dawn greeted by the heavenly chorus of bird life turning thoughts once more towards reproduction. There have been many snowy owl sorties during the intervening months, mostly abortive, but occasionally our efforts have been rewarded with a successful flight, though none so special as the first.

To the uninitiated, the use of a hunting bird to chase and capture prey by a supposed bird-lover may seem in bad taste – even mildly offensive – but the most natural thing in the world for any bird of prey is to search, hunt and kill for its very existence, from the song thrush that tears a worm cruelly from the lawn, to the kingfisher dashing life from a minnow against its riverside perch. The age-old sport of hawking – although the snowy owl can only be regarded as an extreme example of this – is merely sharing the natural instincts of a hunting bird – and until comparatively recently man – to kill for its survival.

While the training and hunting of Phantom has been something of a light-hearted undertaking, and could hardly be taken seriously by even the broadest-minded falconer, it has been the realisation of a boyhood dream, and for that reason alone, a most satisfying and enlightening experience. Looking back on the venture, I have been afforded a privileged glance into the workings of the snowy owl mind and temperament. Often with comical or even disastrous results, I have shared with Phantom the thrills – and spills! – of the chase, to my mind the most natural form of hunting available to present-day man, with the odds stacked heavily in favour of the quarry. The entire venture was a one-off never to be repeated. Upon reflection, I would sooner tackle a whole nestful of young goshawks than undertake the training of another snowy owl.

Or would I? Even as I pen these final lines, Phantom's parents are once again kicking up an unholy shindig every evening, the male calling lustily

Nothing – nobody – could deny us this moment of glory!

from the elevated log in the centre of the displaying ground.

There is also the faintest suggestion of a nesting scrape in the extreme far corner of the aviary.

Antiseptic cream? Hawk glove? Sticking plaster? Bandages? Now just where did I put that dustbin lid ...?

Afterword

At the culmination of my snowy owl training endeavours, Spook and Phantom were transferred to take part in a captive breeding project, where both are apparently doing well.

Both have probably long forgotten their early training exploits, and also their tutor, though the experience will remain with me indefinitely. I wish them well. Any breeding success will be long-term, as the snowy owl rarely produces fertile eggs until at least three years of age. Their parents continue, with varying success, to produce offspring each season, and have managed once to rear a brood without my removing the chicks.